FRANCISCO'S GOLDEN GATE PARK

A Thousand and Seventeen Acres of Stories

CHRISTOPHER POLLOCK

Photography by Erica Katz

Library of Congress Cataloging-in-Publication Data
Pollock, Christopher
        San Francisco's Golden Gate Park : a thousand
    and seventeen acres of stories / text by Christopher
    Pollock ; photography by Erica Katz.
        Includes bibliographical references and index.
        ISBN 1-55868-545-6 (alk. paper)
        1. Golden Gate Park (San Francisco, Calif.)—
    Guidebooks. 2. Golden Gate Park (San Francisco,
    Calif.)—History. 3. Golden Gate Park (San Francisco,
    Calif.)—Pictorial works. 4. San Francisco (Calif.)—
    Building, structures, etc.—Guidebooks. 5. San
    Francisco (Calif.)—Building, structures, etc.—
    Pictorial works. I. Katz, Erica. II. Title
    F869.S37 G646 2001
    979.4'61 – dc21   00-010963

The quoted material in the sidebar on page 96 is from
Don't Call It Frisco by Herb Caen © 1953 by Herb Caen.
Permission of Doubleday, a division of Random House,
Inc.

President/Publisher: Charles M. Hopkins
Editorial Staff: Douglas A. Pfeiffer, Timothy W. Frew,
    Ellen Harkins Wheat, Tricia Brown, Kathy
    Matthews, Jean Andrews, Jean Bond-Slaughter
Production Staff: Richard L. Owsiany, Joanna Goebel
Copy Editor: Barbara Fuller
Design: Elizabeth Watson
Map: Gray Mouse Graphics

Printed in Hong Kong

Without knowing it, Elaine Molinari was a catalyst for this book's inspiration.

Donald Andreini of San Francisco Architectural Heritage contributed valuable advice on several occasions. Several others gave me information about specific sites including: Peter Baye, "Buffalo Phil" Carleton, Debbie Cooper, and Bridget Maley of Architectural Resources Group, Sargent Bob Fitzer of the San Francisco Police Department, Jim Harvey, Sidney Lawrence, Scot Medbury who is the Director of Strybing Arboretum, author Judith Robinson, William L. Ryan, Christopher Ver Planck, Richard G. Turner Jr. of *Pacific Horticulture* magazine, and Thom Weyand.

Ora Schulman of Graphic Arts Center Publishing Company was instrumental in making the book concept come alive to those who sat in a Portland conference room reading the proposal.

And my gratitude to David Wakely for suggesting the publisher.

Very special kudos go to Robert Shepard. More than a literary agent, Robert has been a cheerleader, teacher, and critic. I particularly appreciate his generous and invaluable editorial advice. Several times he went above and beyond the call of duty during the project. I cherish his professional friendship and enthusiasm toward my work.

Reference resources include: The Bancroft Library, University of California at Berkeley; Ellen Harding, California State Library; Deborah Learner and Tom Mrakava, City and County of San Francisco, Recreation and Park Department; The Fine Arts Museums of San Francisco, M. H. de Young Memorial Museum; Helen Crocker Russell Library of Horticulture, Strybing Arboretum; Malliard Library, California Academy of Sciences, National Maritime Museum, San Francisco; Tom Fowler, San Francisco Public Library, General Collections, and Koshland San Francisco History Center; Society of California Pioneers; Sutro Library; and Wells Fargo Bank Historical Services.

I regret that I was not given access to the Ray Clary Golden Gate Park Collection at the Museum of the City of San Francisco, a collection whose contents might have been a contribution to the book.

Golden Gate Park is not just a great urban treasure, a botanical wonder, and a sterling, sylvan retreat in the heart of one of the world's most beautiful cities. It is a living testament to the dreams of man.

The desire to build a large, European-style park in San Francisco 135 years ago was dismissed by most experts as pure political folly. The only space big enough to accommodate such a park was in a vast sandy wilderness known as the "Outside Lands." No less an authority than Frederick Law Olmsted, famed co-designer of Central Park in New York, declared the area "wholly wanting in grace and cheerfulness."

But at least one determined visionary disagreed. And William Hammond Hall's work in surveying the dunes, drawing the topographical maps, and creating the park's sweeping design—transforming a garden oasis out of sand—ranks as one of the great achievements in the history of the West Coast, alongside the construction of the San Francisco Golden Gate and Bay Bridges.

In the past century, the history of San Francisco and the park have become as intertwined as the roots of a grove of redwood trees. Whether serving as a backdrop for the California Midwinter International Exposition in 1894, as a sanctuary for the victims of the 1906 earthquake, as a setting for cultural institutions like the California Academy of Sciences, or as the national symbol for the hippie generation in the '60s, Golden Gate Park has been at the epicenter of the shifting trends and movements that have helped shape the city's soul.

And no matter whether the attraction was free love, free concerts, or freshly planted flowers, the park has been a global magnet, enticing visitors with its myriad charms. In many ways, and to many enterprises, it is a city within a city. More than 15 million people come to experience the park's wonders each year, and tourism officials estimate that the park generates an economic benefit to the city of more than $500 million per year.

Golden Gate Park is a marvel of microclimates and private passions. From weekend soccer games at the Polo Field, to quiet trips to the fly-casting pools, or to festive gatherings like Opera in the Park, the greenbelt carved by master gardener John McLaren offers visitors almost every conceivable recreational pursuit—sometimes to the point of overuse. On any given day, the park is crowded with thousands of joggers, bikers, sunbathers, in-line skaters, golfers, archers, and art lovers.

In recent years, Golden Gate Park has begun to show some of the signs of its age, and it has suffered from many of the same problems that plague the surrounding city: homelessness, crime, traffic woes, and political neglect.

But, as always, the citizens that cherish the park have responded by approving millions in bond money and contributing to private capital campaigns to rebuild its fragile infrastructure and to restore historic gems like the Conservatory of Flowers.

Even naysayers like Olmsted came to admire Golden Gate Park's undeniable beauty. Yet more than any other great urban park, the one-time sea of sand serves as a symbol of San Francisco's fighting spirit. It has survived disasters both natural and man-made, ongoing cultural encroachments, and political battles. But it remains as breathtaking today as it did a century ago.

For no matter how many years pass by, the woodland on the western edge of San Francisco shows the world its wonder: It takes great vision to build a world-class park. It takes great heart to build one for the ages.

—Ken Garcia
San Francisco Chronicle

CONTENTS

1 THE EASTERN END 13

2 THE MUSIC CONCOURSE 51

CONTENTS

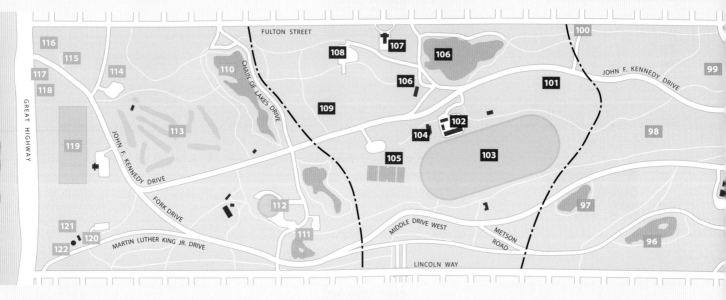

FULTON STREET

107

108

106

106

100

JOHN F. KENNEDY DRIVE

99

110

CHAIN OF LAKES DRIVE

116

115

114

117

118

GREAT HIGHWAY

113

119

JOHN F. KENNEDY DRIVE

FORK DRIVE

109

101

102

104

105

103

98

97

96

112

111

121

120

122

MARTIN LUTHER KING JR. DRIVE

MIDDLE DRIVE WEST

METSON ROAD

LINCOLN WAY

SAN FRANCISCO GOLDEN GATE PARK

GOLDEN GATE BRIDGE

101

Pacific Ocean

SAN FRANCISCO/ OAKLAND BAY BRIDGE

80

San Francisco Bay

GOLDEN GATE PARK

SAN FRANCISCO

1

101

280

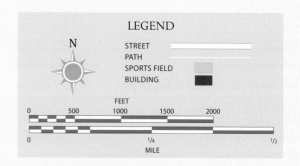

LEGEND

N

STREET	
PATH	
SPORTS FIELD	
BUILDING	

0	500	1000	1500	2000

FEET

0	1/4	1/2

MILE

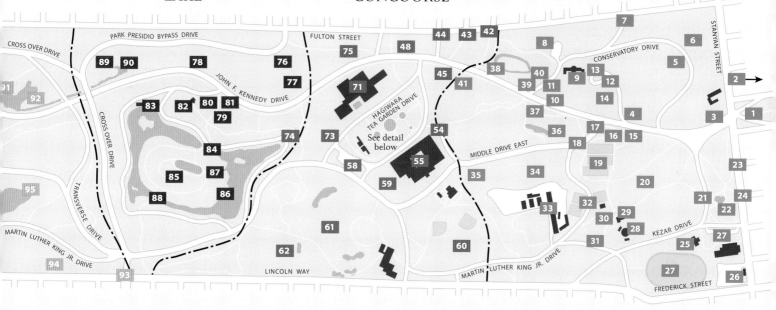

3
STOW LAKE

2
THE MUSIC CONCOURSE

1
THE EASTERN END

CROSS OVER DRIVE

PARK PRESIDIO BYPASS DRIVE

FULTON STREET

STANYAN STREET

7

89 90 78 75 48 44 43 42 8 6 CONSERVATORY DRIVE 5

76 38 40 13 9 12

91 77 JOHN F. KENNEDY DRIVE 45 39 11 2

92 41 10 14

HAGIWARA TEA GARDEN DRIVE 37 4 3 1

83 82 80 81 54 36 17 16 15

CROSS OVER DRIVE 79 73 71 See detail below 18 19 23

84 58 55 MIDDLE DRIVE EAST 35 34 20 21 24

95 85 87 59 33 32 29 22

TRANSVERSE DRIVE 88 86 30 28 27

MARTIN LUTHER KING JR. DRIVE 61 31 25 KEZAR DRIVE 27

94 62 60 26

93 LINCOLN WAY MARTIN LUTHER KING JR. DRIVE 27 FREDERICK STREET

The site numbers on the map correspond with the site numbers in the Contents list (pages 4-5) and in the text.

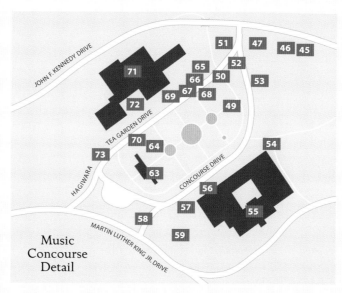

JOHN F. KENNEDY DRIVE

51 47 46 45

71 65 52

66 50 53

69 67 68

72 49

HAGIWARA TEA GARDEN DRIVE 70 64 54

73 63

56

58 57 55

59

MARTIN LUTHER KING JR. DRIVE

CONCOURSE DRIVE

Music Concourse Detail

Every place has a story to tell, and Golden Gate Park—an icon and keystone of San Francisco's park system—is no exception. Millions of people have visited the park over the years, but only a few know of all the rich nuggets that it harbors. Golden Gate Park offers a dizzying array of treasures: fascinating buildings, scenic meadows and lakes, important monuments, and major museums. With all the many hidden foot and bridle paths that traverse the landscape, one veteran member of the mounted police patrol says he has not yet seen all of the park.

The history of Golden Gate Park goes back to the 1860s. The Gold Rush and the discovery of the Comstock Lode in the mid-1800s had catapulted San Francisco from a minor port town into a metropolis, buoyed by completion of the transcontinental railroad in 1869. Pioneer Californians were proud of their isolation in the Far West but were also aware of their difference from the established, cultured East Coast. The emerging cosmopolitan city lacked the earmarks of greatness, such as museums, wide tree-lined boulevards, and monumental civic buildings, let alone a great park.

With the blossoming of large, late-19th-century businesses in San Francisco

Vanished bell tower (see site 41)

came a much more dense population. Businesses created jobs and enticed workers to San Francisco, but they also created crowded conditions. Society sought a balance between the urban and natural worlds and felt a romantic yearning for the simpler past. Everyone could see the need for a remote park to provide an escape from their workaday lives. Parks became an antidote to the materialistic ambitions of the city's citizens.

A quintessential place of outdoor recreation (and re-creation), Golden Gate Park would one day be an important piece of San Francisco's infrastructure, a feature that would help make the West Coast city a distinctive metropolitan area. The park's designer, William Hammond Hall, illustrated the independent spirit of the Bay Area when he ignored the advice of Central Park's landscape architect Frederick Law Olmsted and created an oasis where Olmsted thought none could be built. (San Francisco was also to ignore the Chicago-based Daniel "Make No Little Plans" Burnham's advice to polish the city's image with a grand new street layout, although some aspects of Burnham's thinking, and of Olmsted's, were later incorporated.) Just a generation after the overland wagons and seaworthy ships had delivered their cargoes of pioneers to the City by the Bay, the park was, in varying degrees, covered in greenery.

Few visitors know the story of how the park was created, let alone of the foundation of sand dunes blanketed with trees, shrubbery, and other plants. Seemingly natural oases containing lakes, streams, and waterfalls are cradled within its rolling landscape. Key to creating the verdant appearance of this dry, windy environment has been water. The fact that Golden Gate Park has endured as the playground of the recreation-hungry city is a testament to its visionary founders and hardworking keepers.

The many monuments and buildings constructed in late-19th-century San Francisco were meant to project the accomplishments of American civilization. Post-Gold Rush architecture within the park reflects the eclectic tastes of the Victorian period. Some buildings look to past styles, such as Mission Revival, Classical, and Spanish Colonial. Themed buildings redolent of Egypt, Holland, Spain, England, Italy, and other countries were built in neohistorical styles as America was finding its own way stylistically. There were constructions in the rustic taste: bridges across the Chain of Lakes and several shelters using all manners of branches and logs.

At the turn of the century, Golden Gate Park was the free Disneyland of its time, with attractions ranging from animals and birds to lush plantings and numerous types of recreational and athletic activities. It was a huge success, despite its location far from where the populace lived. Competition came from other nearby commercial ventures, including the closer-to-downtown Woodward's Gardens in the Mission District (the city's playground—for a fee, 1866–92); the first Chutes, located on Haight Street between Cole and Clayton Streets (an amusement park, 1895–1901); and its second version at Tenth Avenue and Fulton Street (1902–08); and several incarnations of Playland-at-the-Beach (1916–72). Of these places, only the park has held up against the city's hunger for homesites.

Many structures that today contribute to the texture of the park were never planned by its originators, who preferred to keep development to a minimum. Furthermore, like old growth in a forest, many of the park's earliest structures have been replaced by updated versions or removed entirely. In a way, Golden Gate Park is an anachronism, a relic of the Industrial Revolution's pinnacle, the Gilded Age. It echoes many of the major events and figures of any city: the dawn of flight, earthquake and fire, expositions, war, presidential visits, movie stars, politics, moneyed donors, and just plain citizens. In the park's early years, society focused on the idea of progress, and the park's architecture reflected that notion with major innovations in structure. Its texture, interwoven with the names of the city's builders during a time of dynamic change, is a reflection of San Francisco's enterprising characters and evolution into a premiere metropolitan city.

Citizens have recently taken a more active interest in the park's preservation, approving millions of their tax and bond dollars to repair the failing infrastructure. Aging lighting, water delivery, and sewage removal systems are being replaced. Major storms in 1995 did considerable damage to the park, including the historic Conservatory of Flowers, which is being fully restored with public and private funds. Replacement of the de Young Museum and rebuilding of the California Academy of Sciences, changes that will dramatically revise the landscape of the park's Music Concourse, have been under consideration for many years and are now moving forward.

I was inspired to start this work in earnest more than five years ago. A friend, Elaine Molinari, then working at the Recreation and Park Department, related to me some of the fascinating stories of the park's creation. With my interest in history, it occurred to me that this would be a great book project.

As I sought out available publications, I sensed a need for an updated and cohesive approach to all of the park's physical buildings and sites. The earliest book I know on the topic is F. F. Byington's *Official Guide to Golden Gate Park of San Francisco* (1894), published by the Board of Park Commissioners, probably for the 1894 California Midwinter International Exposition (known as the Midwinter Fair). C. R. Lippmann's *Trip through Internationally Famous Golden Gate Park* (1937) is also informative. My favorite publication, because of its depth and numerous photographs, is Guy and Helen Giffen's *Story of Golden Gate Park* (1949). The most in-depth work is Raymond Clary's two-volume *The Making of Golden Gate Park*, published between 1980 and 1987, primarily written as a chronological description of events.

The many earlier publications that I uncovered provided a basis on which I could work, but I wanted to dig deeper. My greatest pleasures in putting together this book have been in correcting previous misinformation and in revealing little-known facts. As I researched information about the various sites, anomalies surfaced, and in many instances I found little or no information at all. A city-sponsored publication attributed the Amundsen Memorial to artist F. Asbjornsen, for example—but I could find no biographical information about the artist, and was startled when I went to the site to read the name of Hans W. Jauchen on the plaque! My longest and most obsessive search centered around the designer for the Phoebe Apperson Hearst fountain. After contacting many people and following several leads over a two-year period, I randomly searched *Building and Engineering News*, where I finally found the payoff (though the actual date of the fountain's installation remains unclear). Unrealized grand schemes that would have been out of scale with the park were also revealed, such as a stadium designed by Reid Brothers architects, George Applegarth's gate for the Sharpe Estate, and a Breon Archway (other than the one built).

Photographic research revealed much as well: while poring over historic photographs, I was surprised to find that the Goethe and Schiller Monument is not placed where it was originally dedicated. Old maps revealed another site for the Starr King monument. The Sweeney Observatory was noted in one publication to be built of brick, not concrete. A plaque on the Brown Gate implies that Beardslee bequest monies funded it, but in fact, that money was used only to widen the roadway later on.

The Ghirardelli Card Shelter, now a shadow of what it once was, had little press when it was built. With the assistance of family descendants, I fleshed out the story—but a photograph of the original incarnation of the Shelter has eluded me. The Senior Center was attributed to Emil de Neuf, a city architect who had died 15 years before the building was constructed. I solved the mystery by looking through *all* of the drawings in the Recreation and Park Department's archive related to the park, an arduous but revealing task. I still don't know who designed the Rustic Bridge over Stow Lake, or what the piece of sculpture was that once sat at the base of Huntington Falls.

This book is a hybrid of a guide, a history, and a photographic journey. It is organized so that you may visit all of the park's sites in sequence from east to west. The tour follows the park's meandering paths and roads, with visits to *all* of the park's features, not just the popular ones. Interwoven with the site descriptions are boxes containing tidbits of the fascinating related stories. More extensive sidebars give information about related people, events, and historical trends—the history of parks in the United States; the stories of William Hammond Hall and John McLaren, the park's first two superintendents; and the effects of the 1906 San Francisco earthquake and fire, for example.

The six chapters cover areas loosely defined by boundaries. Chapter 1, "The Eastern End," covers the oldest part of the park, virtually unchanged since its beginnings, with a boundary about where building construction was initially intended to stop. Chapter 2, "The Music Concourse," covers the cultural heart of the park—the museums, arboretum, and many of the park's statues—with roots going back to the 1894 California Midwinter International Exposition. Highway Route 1 provides a boundary for chapter 3, "Stow Lake," (an artificially landscaped area of water and woods). Chapter 4, "West of Cross Over Drive," includes mostly open meadow and woodland features. The boundary between chapters 5 and 6 parallels Chain of Lakes Drive. Chapter 5, "The Golden Gate Park Stadium," covers an area devoted primarily to active outdoor sports. Finally, Chapter 6, "Facing West," covers the western boundary of the park along the Pacific Ocean.

Many of the sites described in this book can be viewed and enjoyed at any time, for no fee. For those with restricted access, practical information follows the site description in italic type. Included are contact numbers and Web sites, hours of visitation (if any), and fees (if any). For general information about the park, including information regarding accessibility, call the Recreation and Park Department at 415/831-2700. John F. Kennedy Drive is closed to cars on Sundays from the McLaren Lodge to Highway 1; visitors are welcome on foot, bicycle, roller blades, or other modes of travel during that time. Historical site designations, if any, also follow the site descriptions.

As new generations of San Franciscans and visitors to the City by the Bay seek a sanctuary from the frenetic pace of the Technology Age, Golden Gate Park is more necessary and relevant than ever before; it still soothes the distraught edges of our lives. *San Francisco's Golden Gate Park: A Thousand and Seventeen Acres of Stories* celebrates the activities and places the city's backyard has to offer. There is a lot to see and learn . . . so, Happy Touring!

Side view of vanished suspension bridge. Blueprint, from John Roebling drawing.

❧ THE EASTERN END ❧

Just as the Golden Gate Strait welcomed early tourists to San Francisco Bay long ago, so Golden Gate Park's downtown-oriented eastern third acts as a portal through which many San Franciscans and tourists venture to rekindle their city-weary spirits. Consequently, many of the park's attractions are located in this highly visible, manicured, and most-visited area of the park. Yet, as accessible as the east end is today, the lack of roads and transportation made it seem far from the city's population center when Golden Gate Park was first proposed, bringing much criticism from those who couldn't imagine that San Francisco would ever grow beyond its early borders.

In 1870, the park's planner and first superintendent, William Hammond Hall, started work on the 270 acres located at the eastern end, including the 275-foot-wide Panhandle. The early plan called for an east end graced with a playground, 25-acre picnic site, music concourse, and conservatory. This area was considered to be the genteel part of the acreage, compared to the wild western portion facing the turbulent Pacific. Unlike much of the rest of the park, the eastern end remains virtually as it was first laid out.

◀ *Australian Tree Fern Dell with Lily Pond*   ▲ *William Hammond Hall*

1 The Panhandle

In San Francisco, "Panhandle" refers not to the northern extension of Texas but rather to the 23.4 acres that serve as a welcome mat to Golden Gate Park.

Bounded on its eight-block length by the major automobile arteries of Fell and Oak Streets, the Panhandle is perhaps most famous as a hangout for hippies during the 1967 Summer of Love. Ghostly echoes of folk music resound from the Flower Power Generation that once rallied here. Lined with large Victorian-era homes, the spreading lawn with its winding paths is an excellent place for strolling, skating, or bicycle riding. It also has a basketball court named in 2000 to honor NBA legend Nate Thurmond and a children's playground.

Originally called The Avenue, the Panhandle dates to 1871. It once provided curving carriageways, which carried auto traffic after 1912. Originally, Ashbury and Cole Streets crossed the strip but, in 1915, these crossroads were closed. Limiting the growing city's cross-connections soon became a civic issue, with the upshot that Masonic Avenue was extended through by a voter-approved ordinance in 1920.

Dramatic changes to the Panhandle occurred in the 1950s: on July 1, 1953,

> 1 A property was being sought for the newly created San Francisco Junior College during Depression-strapped 1935. Citizen Charles F. Gerughty suggested using part of the Panhandle, which would spare the city the cost of property acquisition, with the added benefit that the park's Kezar Stadium and Big Rec could also be used. The letter to the *San Francisco Chronicle's* editor contended that "this strip of land could be put to a useful purpose without detracting in any way from the beauty of the Park itself." Nothing came of the notion.

Oak and Fell Streets, along its northern and southern borders, were converted to one-way streets; then, on February 10, 1955, the curving roadways within the Panhandle were transformed for pedestrian use.

In fact, early plans called for an even wider Panhandle, bounded on the north by Fulton Street and on the south by Haight Street.

Another expansion scheme, proposed by Mayor James Duval Phelan in 1899, advocated extending the strip to the Civic Center. Phelan planned to transform San Francisco into a metropolitan star, using Paris as the model. This same concept was used in the monumentally conceived but ill-fated 1905 Burnham Plan, published just before the 1906 earthquake and fire. That proposal was to extend the strip eastward to the Civic Center, then continue it on to the shore of San Francisco Bay.

Features of the design were a sunken grade (an idea Frederick Law Olmsted had proposed for Van Ness Avenue), with the perpendicular streets of Divisadero and Fillmore continuing across the greenbelt (with Fillmore carried on a grand bridge). City Engineer M. M. O'Shaughnessy urged the idea in a report to the Board of Public Works again in 1930, one of many occasions when the idea was considered—but the extension has never materialized.

2 William McKinley Monument

William McKinley, 25th U.S. president, died on September 14, 1901, after being shot by anarchist Leon Czolgosz. Four months prior to that, on May 12, McKinley had made a highly successful visit to San Francisco, creating a bond with the city's citizens.

Nine sculptors submitted proposals for this statue to honor McKinley, all using only native California materials, and their designs were shown in the 1902 Spring Exhibition of the Mark Hopkins Institute of Art. Robert Ingersoll Aitken,

The Development of Urban Parks in America

The concept of an American public park did not come of age until the 19th century. Some ideas for such places came from France and England, but American priorities and traditions were combined with these earlier concepts to create entirely new kinds of urban spaces.

Urban parks certainly are nothing new. Social historian Lewis Mumford cited an early urban park surrounding the Imperial palaces of Rome, but this pleasure ground was meant for the compound's occupants. Julius Caesar opened his gardens to the general public, the earliest such gesture recorded, but they served only the immediate area—which was populated by affluent citizens.

In medieval and early modern England, a park was an enclosed tract of land owned by royals or well-to-do commoners and used for viewing or sport shooting of animals. In 1652, paying guests were admitted to the royal grounds of London's Hyde Park, a romanticized bit of country within the congested city. During the 18th century, several designers of British estates influenced early public parks with their deceptively natural-appearing landscapes. Noted early English landscape designers Lancelot "Capability" Brown and Humphrey Repton skillfully disguised

human intervention in their artificially constructed scenic landscapes.

John Claudius Loudon's Arboretum (1840) in Derby, England, was one of the first public parks in Britain created specifically so that common people could "enjoy a rare opportunity of expanding their minds by contemplation of nature." London's Kew Gardens, Kensington Gardens, and Hyde Park were opened to the public by the mid-1800s. French-born Jean-Charles-Adolphe Alphand later contributed to the movement with his transformation, in concert with Baron Georges Eugene von Haussmann, of the Bois de Boulogne in Paris from a hunting park into an English-style pastoral landscape (1852–70).

Meanwhile, a distinctly American vernacular was taking shape in New England, based on the centrally located village greens that had been part of English villages since medieval times. Frequently the green had a water well, a livestock watering pond, and public corrections, including a jail, stocks, and a whipping post. The church and market might be here, too. Commons, such as Boston Common (1630), were created for shared utilitarian purposes, including military exercises, public assembly, and the grazing of cattle. Later, across the street from Boston Common, visitors

strolled among more refined floral displays in the Public Garden. Still later, visionary James Oglethorpe created a plan for Savannah, Ga., that set aside green squares surrounded by residences and institutions (1733)—though not for the lower class.

Soon after the American Revolution, civic improvement programs brought popularity to New England town centers and commons. Public subscription financed the elm-shaded New Haven Green (1787) in Connecticut, and in 1815, five acres in Philadelphia were landscaped and opened as a public garden, the beginnings of Fairmount Park—at 4,180 acres, one of the largest municipal park systems in the world.

Garden cemeteries were cousin to the parks. Here kin could be buried and immortalized, and here, too, friends and family could share a picnic in a romantic pastoral landscape. Mortality rates were still quite high, and these sprawling landscapes replaced tightly spaced church graveyards and burying grounds and suited the Victorian custom of remaining close to the dead. The first of its kind was Mt. Auburn Cemetery (1831) in Cambridge, Massachusetts, a monument-studded sylvan retreat that soon set the standard for garden cemetery taste. Kensal Green Cemetery in London inspired John

Notman to design Philadelphia's 20-acre Laurel Hill (1836); it and 178-acre Greenwood (1838) in Brooklyn, New York, survive as prime examples, including winding paths and naturalistic water features. The garden cemetery had its heyday in the 1840s and 1850s, but after that, park fashions changed, and the association with mortality that had earlier been fashionable began to limit its appeal.

A new ideal of setting aside vast tracts for conservation was emerging. In the national picture, eastern California's then-remote and difficult-to-access Yosemite Valley was established as a state park (1864), paving the way for the concept of a national park system. Yellowstone, in northwestern Wyoming, became the first national park in 1872, followed by California's Yosemite and Sequoia in 1890. The conservation of open space signaled that a life *in* nature resulted in moral and societal benefits.

As did household gardens. Beginning probably in the 14th century, such gardens were initially designed to feed or provide medicinal plants for the family. Later, they became aesthetic havens as well. George Washington's garden at Mt. Vernon was significant for its style and variety. Large, elaborate gardens for fruits, vegetables, and flowers, such as the one at Chateau Villandry in the Loire Valley

of France, is formal yet also functional.

With urban density on the rise, a city's infrastructure demanded a larger proportion of open space. Furthermore, the many time-saving amenities of the Industrial Revolution provided more leisure time. Fresh air was considered to be a means for preventing epidemics of disease, common prior to the rise of modern medicine in the 20th century. Americans built urban parks to escape "to the country," even if limited transportation meant "the country" was near at hand. The democratic idea of a space to be shared by all classes, intended to elevate the personal and public character of all urban dwellers (especially the working class), emerged. A park provided opportunities for fresh air, healthy exercise, and pleasurable diversion.

Hudson Valley-bred Andrew Jackson Downing is considered to be the first important teacher of American landscape design. Downing, the son of a nurseryman, paraphrased English picturesque landscape theories and was more an arbiter of taste than an originator in the field. A prolific writer, Downing is credited with forming the basis of landscape design theory in America. It was he who promoted the notion of a great park for New York City in 1851—but with his early death,

at age 37, his teachings were silenced.

Prior to Central Park, New York City had enjoyed small gated parks such as Gramercy Park and St. John's Place Park—but these were private. In March 1858, New York held a competition to design what would be the first true American urban public park. The winning entry was from Frederick Law Olmsted and the English-born Calvert Vaux. Vaux had invited Olmsted to participate in the competition after reading Olmsted's book *Walks and Talks of an American Farmer in England*. Despite his lack of a college education, Olmsted could call upon a formidable knowledge of soils and agriculture. As the highly visible architect-in-chief of the park's construction, his democratic social convictions and keen sense of the land helped him fulfill the needs of city dwellers. Initially called *Greensward*, the park is now the 843-acre Central Park, the largest preserved refuge in the most populous city in the world. With its completion in 1876, a whole movement began. Thereafter, landscape architecture throughout the United States was seen as a complex art form.

A broader definition of what constituted a park evolved with new tastes and pastimes. Outdoor sports grew in popularity during the latter half of the 19th century, for example, when technology and the eight-hour workday gave workers more free time. Several firsts occurred for organized professional sports, including the formation of the first American golf club in 1887, the first pro football game in 1895, and the first World Series for baseball in 1903. One by one, fields for these specific pastimes were added to parks. The park now provided space not only for a passive recreational experience, but also for active recreational sports.

With their acceptance, parks in U.S. cities grew beyond a pastoral grove or meadow. Purists would have kept out the vulgar elements—structures, athletic fields, roads—but ultimately, parks have become a synthesis of popular culture, including pleasure *and* recreation. *Common, cemetery, town square, open space, garden*—all have led up to the urban park.

who won the commission after a second round, had also sculpted the notable statue atop the Dewey Monument in Union Square. The McKinley Monument was originally scheduled to be erected at the prominent intersection of Van Ness Avenue and Market Street, but that location was discarded. San Francisco citizens paid the cost of $30,000.

The McKinley Monument features an inset marble bas-relief plaque of McKinley set into a 15-foot-high pedestal on a stepped granite podium 45 feet in diameter. It is one of three presidential

2 On October 6, 1966, some 500 people, mostly young, attended a gathering in the park's Panhandle to protest a new state law making it illegal to possess the hallucinogenic drug LSD. Flags decorated with stylized marijuana leaves flew overhead at the gathering, billed as a Love Pageant Rally. Rock bands, including Big Brother and the Holding Company, blared music as the crowd sang and danced in a drug-induced haze. It was one of the first mass protests on a piece of land that would become famous for such protests.

William McKinley Monument

2 President Theodore Roosevelt's 1903 visit to the park was to have lasting importance for the entire state. After visiting San Francisco, the president camped in Yosemite with naturalist John Muir for four days, where the primary topic was conservation. The eventual result was to expand federal protection of extraordinary land areas, such as Yosemite, by proclaiming the sites national monuments. During the trip, Roosevelt also gave the commencement address and inaugurated the Hearst Greek Theater at the University of California in Berkeley and dedicated the Dewey Monument in Union Square.

monuments in the park, all honoring Ohio-born presidents (the others are devoted to James Abram Garfield and Ulysses S. Grant).

The polished bronze spade used by McKinley's successor, Theodore Roosevelt, to break ground for the monument on May 13, 1903, was a copy of the spade McKinley had used to break ground for the Dewey Monument in Union Square. Dedicated on November 24, 1904, this statue was a powerful reminder of the tragedy that had catapulted the brash and confident Roosevelt to the office of president.

3 **McLaren Lodge and Uncle John's Tree**

The mother ship of the park, McLaren Lodge stands framed by a green lawn, giving visitors a taste of the meadows and dells scattered throughout the park. Officially named McLaren Lodge by the park's board of commissioners in February 1943, the lodge is the headquarters of the park. With its construction completed in 1896, it originally served a dual purpose: as

Courtyard garden behind McLaren Lodge

3 In 1900, Mayor James Duval Phelan proposed that the park's four-year-old McLaren Lodge be decommissioned and used as a branch library. The mayor intended to move the park commissioners to city hall so that he could more closely watch their activities. The *San Francisco Call* newspaper stated that this was a "fantastic freak notion," and others agreed; the plan was vetoed. In 1986, Supervisor Carol Ruth Silver proposed a scheme to use the historic structure as the mayor's official residence. Nothing came of that idea, either.

headquarters of the San Francisco Parks Department and as the superintendent's home, with a separate entry. (Before its completion, a stick-style building across the street had served the purpose.) Park Superintendent John McLaren, his wife Jane, and their family lived in the west portion, containing six bedrooms; the east side contained offices and the commissioners' meeting room. After McLaren's death on January 12, 1943, Julius Leon Girod was appointed superintendent. His family resided at the lodge until May 12, 1950, when they moved out so that the newly combined Recreation and Park Department, two separate entities up to that

The Greening of the Outside Lands: The Park's Early History

Today's tapestry of buildings, meadows, lakes, athletic fields, forests, and gardens is far from the original state of the northwest tip of the San Francisco peninsula, for which a more appropriate name would have been "Sand Francisco." Labeled the "Great Sand Bank" on an 1853 map, the sparsely populated and virtually treeless landscape of windswept, rolling dunes gave no hint of the potential for greenery. Naysayers called the park's future location a "dreary desert"; indeed, the chosen spot must have seemed the most undesirable area imaginable to those without a trained sense of landscaping. What was to become Golden Gate Park was an unprecedented horticultural experiment on a vast scale.

Early chronicler Frank Soulé noted in his 1854 *Annals of San Francisco*, "There seems no provision . . . for a public park—the true lungs of a large city." Soulé scolded that every *square vara* (the Spanish unit of measure still in use at the time) was slated for building lots. In addition to Portsmouth Square, San Francisco's original nucleus, only three squares had been planned as recreation space for the town. The three earliest maps of the city—by surveyors Jean-Jacques Vioget (1839), Jasper O'Farrell (1847), and William M. Eddy (1849)—had projected only two additional open spaces: Union Square and Washington Square, both gifts to the city in 1850 from John White Geary, the first mayor of newly American San Francisco. Columbia Square was a third. Later, in 1855, the Western Addition was planned with seven large squares. San Francisco swelled from a population of some 1,000 in 1848 to more than 149,400 by 1870. Rapid growth left little time for planning parks.

During that time, financier William "Billy" Chapman Ralston persuaded the board of supervisors to bring noted East Coast landscape designer Frederick Law Olmsted to San Francisco to advise about the possibilities of a grand park on the western section of the peninsula.

Olmsted had teamed with architect Calvert Vaux to win a competition in 1858 to create New York's highly successful Central Park. In 1865, San Francisco Mayor Henry Perrin Coon contacted Olmsted about preparing a similar plan for his city, but Olmsted did not believe that such an oasis could be created on the arid Outside Lands. Instead, he proposed a greenbelt (an Olmsted trademark used in several other U.S. cities) that would stretch through the city from Aquatic Park to the vicinity of Duboce Park. He chose sites—especially along Van Ness Avenue—that were sheltered, which he felt was intrinsic to the success of landscaping with native drought-tolerant materials, a visionary idea at that time. The long-range concept could be extended into a series of small parks over time. Ultimately, Olmsted's plan was not adopted, because city fathers had hoped for something more like Central Park. Olmsted's ideas did greatly influence the supervisors in their decision to proceed with a park, however.

Acquisition of land for the park was a long, drawn-out matter. When San Francisco petitioned the Board of Land Commissioners for land that was not originally within the city limits, a legal fight ensued to capture the entire west side of the peninsula, bordered by Divisadero Street. Squatters who occupied this desolate area, called the Outside Lands, claimed ownership by possession. Some of these occupants were politically and financially well connected, which helped them stall any movement by the city to claim land they felt they owned as homesteaders. In 1864, U.S. Supreme Court Justice Stephen Johnson Field handed down a decree in favor of the city, which an act of Congress confirmed on March 8, 1866. Although these were steps in the right direction, neither action settled the issue of specific claims. Mayor-Elect Frank McCoppin finally negotiated a settlement, asking claimants to surrender 10 percent of their holdings and help the city acquire the land once and for all.

In 1868, Mayor McCoppin ordered a survey of potential park sites west of Divisadero Street. The state legislature approved order 800 by San Francisco's board of supervisors, and Governor Henry H. Haight signed the bill on December 7, 1868. A committee appointed by the board of supervisors was given the task to appraise and apportion the land; the 1,013 acres established for the park were valued at $801,593. An April 4, 1870, act of the state legislature set the park's boundaries and proclaimed the inception of Golden Gate Park, which was the first documented use of the name. Shortly thereafter, on April 19, the governor appointed a three-person Board of Park Commissioners. Bonds were sold and bids sought for a survey of the future park, a task carried out by William Hammond Hall.

With the land finally in hand, construction started that fall on the area closest to the city, the Panhandle, at the park's eastern end. The process of reclamation was arduous and long but paid off in the end. Hall was well versed in soil management, though he had to be creative to solve the particular problems

associated with converting the park's sometimes shifting sands into a growing medium. To those who argued that the entire park site should be flattened— including one self-serving contractor who coveted the resulting soil as free fill for a project at Mission Bay—Hall recalled Frederick Law Olmsted's advice to capitalize on the "genius of the place" and maintain the site's natural features wherever possible.

The sandy soil posed another challenge when it came time to plant. Lupine (a perennial shrub) was initially planted in the sand dunes but could not take hold fast enough to restrain the blowing sand, especially at the exposed beach areas. Serendipity finally helped: barley grain spilled onto the sand from a horse's feed bag, and Hall noticed later that it had sprouted. The quick-growing seed was broadcast on the sands but lived only a couple of months, not long enough to set deep roots. Next came sea bent grass mixed with yellow lupine. Over this were spread topsoil, manure, and organic matter. By 1873, the drifting sands at the beach had been tamed and further harnessed with a fence made of boards and posts covered with tree boughs and brush. The fence was located about 100 feet from the shoreline and extended across the length of Ocean

Beach to barricade the encroaching winds.

In an 1873 report to the park commissioners, Hall deftly noted, "These enterprises are found to pay—to yield to the city a direct moneyed return on her investment." B. E. Lloyd's *Lights and Shades in San Francisco* notes that just four years after opening, the park, "traversed by promenades, bridle paths and drives, invites the pedestrian, equestrian, or driver to follow their mazy windings into the labyrinths of hedges and borders." Some 15,000 people visited the park that year. By 1876, development had reached Conservatory Valley, despite budget cutbacks.

By the late 1880s, several streetcar lines made the park accessible to all who could afford the fare, boosting its popularity. Railroad tycoon Leland Stanford began conversion of the Market Street Railroad to cable in 1883, increasing the speed and distance of mass transit. The McAllister and Haight Street cable-driven lines brought people to the eastern end of the park for recreation, which in turn made the area a fashionable and sought-after residential district. "Cable, electric and steam-cars reach the park from all parts of the city," noted an 1892 writer. Nine streetcar lines terminated at the park by 1900, providing ample transportation. By 1902, the automobile was also bringing people to the park, but the newfangled method of transportation was initially banned from the park itself because the fast and noisy machines were believed to frighten horses and bicyclists. Finally, in 1904, cars were admitted into the park through the Page Street Gate, although they remained banned from the Concourse until 1912.

Transformed or not, the arid, sandy environment of the park couldn't sustain plants without a constant supply of fresh water. The Spring Valley Water Company had supplied the park's lifeblood for its first seven years, but water cost money, even at the reduced rate the city paid, and the park commission sought a water supply within the park as early as 1886. The ingenious solution was to drill wells near the salty Pacific Ocean—the first suitable one in 1888, followed by two others—pumped by windmills.

By the turn of the century, the park was already well under way to becoming a special place when it received another boost: a 1900 city charter reform transferred power from the three-person governor-appointed board to a city and county of San Francisco five-member park commission, providing closer contact with the park's development and the needs of San Francisco.

time, could occupy the entire building.

Architect Edward R. Swain designed the Victorian Romanesque-style lodge, clad in three colors of sandstone laid in a broken ashlar pattern. All of the structure's materials were specified to be of California origin. The stone came from a quarry at 26th and Douglass Streets in the Noe Valley District. Other materials include Mission-style red tiles to cap the roof and exposed stained pine. The recessed porch covers a heavily paneled oak door decorated with brass trim. Matching paneling lines the porch interior.

Featured in the lodge is the dark, typically Victorian commissioners' meeting room with mahogany beams and woodwork framing pigskin-clad walls and ceiling panels with decorative brass nails. A working fireplace warms the room. Replacing the original chandeliers are appropriate fixtures from a contemporary church in Birmingham, England, a donation by the Victorian Alliance. Oak parquet laid in a decorative pattern borders the oak strip flooring.

Presiding over the board room is a life-size portrait of McLaren painted by Arthur James Cahill in 1921. It is the property of the Palace of the Legion of Honor and has been on loan since 1943, a gift to the city by Alma de Bretteville

Spreckels, wife of Adolph Bernard Spreckels. The room is open to the public when not in use for meetings.

An unsympathetic modernist annex was constructed in 1950 to house more staff, an upshot of the mergence of the Recreation and Park Departments. Architects Donald B. Kirby and Thomas B. Mulvin designed the two-story building. A glassed-in walkway connects the two buildings. A sensitively integrated access ramp, using cast concrete to look like the original stone, was completed in 1999 and leads to the lodge's front door.

Swain was also the supervising architect to complete the Ferry Building

3 An unfortunately timed phone call from a reporter informed Park Superintendent Julius Leon Girod and his family that they would have to move out of the McLaren Lodge so that the newly combined Recreation and Park Department could move in. The *San Francisco Examiner* called during the family's annual Christmas party in 1949, asking for comment on the family's having to leave their $50-per-month residence by May 1 of the following year. No one in the bureaucracy had informed the Girods of the situation. The family spent a sad holiday—their last at the historic lodge.

(1903) after the untimely death of its 35-year-old designer Arthur Page Brown. Swain designed the sandstone Whittier Mansion in Pacific Heights (1896) and the now-demolished Mechanical Arts Building at the Midwinter Fair.

The area directly in front of the lodge is dedicated to the memory of Recreation and Park General Manager Tom Malloy, who served from 1980 to 1985.

Located on the front lawn of the lodge is Uncle John's Tree. The approximately 100-foot-tall Monterey cypress *(Cupressus macrocarpa)* is the official tree of the city and county of San Francisco. No one knows who planted Uncle John's Tree or how old it is. As its species name implies, its natural habitat is the Monterey Peninsula. The tree is strung with lights for the Christmas season and lit on December 20 (John McLaren's birthday), a tradition started in 1929 as a promotion for Christmas trees.

A very tall specimen of swamp cypress *(Taxodium distichum)* is located just west of the lodge. Each winter, several citizens call the park, alarmed by what appears to be a dead evergreen species—but it is, in fact, a deciduous tree.

City and County of San Francisco Landmark 175.
Location: *501 Stanyan St.*

Tenacious Visionaries: William Hammond Hall and John McLaren

Two men with distinctly different styles share the credit for the creation of Golden Gate Park: engineer William Hammond Hall, for the park's framework and initial landscaping, and horticulturist John McLaren, who made the park his personal mission until his death. McLaren's long tenure often overshadows Hall's expertise, but the determined efforts of both men led to what exists today.

The family of Maryland-born William Hammond Hall (1846–1934) moved to San Francisco in 1853 but relocated to Stockton the next year, following major property losses in one of the city's all-too-common catastrophic fires. "Ham" attended a private academy in Stockton with the intention of attending the military academy at West Point, but with the commencement of the Civil War, his parents revised his plans, and he remained at the academy in Stockton until 1865. His professional civil engineering career started immediately when he apprenticed as a draftsman and surveyor for the U.S. Corps of Engineers. He advanced quickly, among other things surveying the west coast around San Francisco Bay for the U.S. Coast Survey. His efforts with the army allowed him to observe the reclamation of sand dunes along the city's western edge—an important ingredient in his future. With his move to private practice, Hall was on the brink of what would become a renowned, if checkered, career.

On April 19, 1870, Governor Henry H. Haight appointed a three-person Board of Park Commissioners, which soon solicited bids for a topographical survey for a large city park in San Francisco. The 24-year-old Hall won the contract for $4,860 on August 8, 1870, and completed the task, including a preliminary plan, in six months. Hall's prior knowledge of the terrain was an enormous help, as he designed undulating roadways that took advantage of the terrain, kept speeding drivers at bay, and sheltered users from the incessant winds. Appointed superintendent on August 14, 1871, at a salary of $250 a month, Hall met great opposition from naysayers who felt that the Herculean task of turning sand dunes into a verdant park sounded like alchemy.

Later, Hall became a victim of political maneuvering and revenge by former-blacksmith-turned-Assemblyman D. C. Sullivan. Hall had fired Sullivan for padding his bill while in the position of blacksmith, and Sullivan accused Hall of wrongdoing and had him investigated by a special committee. Although none of the charges stuck, Hall resigned in April 1876 when his salary was cut in half. He continued to consult on behalf of the park without compensation, and regained an official title when Governor George Stoneman appointed him consulting engineer to the park in 1886; he kept the position until 1889. During this time, he hired and trained John McLaren as assistant superintendent, initially assigning McLaren the job of landscaping the Children's Quarters, designed by Hall.

Legendary John Hays McLaren (1846–1943) presided over the park as its superintendent for 53 years. Hailing from a farm in Stirling, Scotland, just west of the Firth of Forth, the stocky Scot learned his trade by working on nearby estates from the age of 16. Later he worked in Edinburgh's Royal Botanical Gardens. At age 24, he sailed for America. A short time after arriving on the east coast in 1869, he proceeded to the west coast by ships and by a train across the Isthmus of Panama. Finally settling in San Mateo County, McLaren worked on large estates for 15 years before joining the park. He was employed primarily on the lavish George H. Howard Estate, "El Cerrito," and did work for other notables, such as financier William Chapman Ralston, railroad tycoon Leland Stanford, and banker Darius Ogden Mills. He is responsible for the continuous rows of eucalyptus trees that still line El Camino Real along the peninsula.

Following three years as assistant superintendent, McLaren became superintendent in 1890, overseeing 40 gardeners whose ranks would swell to 400 during his long tenure. Using experience and direct observation, the shrewd and aggressive superintendent worked diligently to keep politics and commercialism out of the park. He was held in great esteem but was also considered hard to work for by some. "Wild game is coming" was the muffled cry when McLaren came to inspect his workers. McLaren's landscaping philosophy was similar to Hall's: he wanted to create a natural look by working with nature, not against it. He was an experienced horticulturist and forester who studied the local climate and what would thrive in it. Still a dynamo when he reached his 70th birthday in 1916, he was granted a special honor. With McLaren's mandatory retirement at hand, the board of supervisors passed special ordinances giving him lifetime tenure over the park. Blind at the end of his life, he relied on protégé Julius Girod to be his eyes.

McLaren's work was not limited to Golden Gate Park but also included other emerging city parks and special events. He did landscaping for the 1915 Panama–Pacific International Exposition (PPIE) and for the 1939 Golden Gate Exposition on Treasure Island. In appreciation, a special day was set aside at the PPIE to honor McLaren for his design work, and two local newspapers presented him with an engraved trophy (a "loving cup"); some 4,000 San Franciscans had contributed as little as a few cents each toward the gift.

Other accolades for the indomitable, self-described "Boss Gardener" included the naming of an avenue in the prestigious Seacliff District after him, and the award of an honorary doctorate by the University of California at Berkeley. Upon his 80th birthday and his 40th year with the park, a 450-acre park in the Outer Mission was named after him. McLaren Lodge in Golden Gate Park honors his long-time contributions, and the East Bay's Tilden Park has a meadow named after him.

After his death in 1943, at age 96, McLaren's body lay in state in the San Francisco City Hall Rotunda, a tribute reserved for very few San Franciscans. Later, the funeral cortege drove his casket through Golden Gate Park, also a special honor, as the park commission normally discouraged corteges from entering the park. His final resting place is, appropriately, the garden cemetery of Cypress Lawn in Colma.

4 Peacock Meadow

This verdant, enclosed meadow, a place where resident peacocks once displayed their elaborate plumage, was established sometime before 1893. The meadow was originally enclosed by "a neat iron fence" that also corralled a small number of Persian sheep. Framing it is the Bowles Collection of Rhododendrons, given by Mary A. McNear Bowles of Piedmont in 1929 in memory of her husband, Philip Ernest Bowles. Most are Himalayan hybrids.

5 Fuchsia Dell

Originally called the Golden Gate Fuchsia Grove, this garden in the park was created by the Recreation and Park Department and dedicated in 1940. Little is known of its early history, but the original plantings may have come from the 1939 Golden Gate International Exposition, noted for the fuchsias featured in some of its landscaping. Park Superintendent John McLaren was a special adviser to the fair commission and was known to have recycled many of its plantings from the Panama–Pacific International Exposition to the park many years earlier.

The world's first fuchsia-specific organization, the American Fuchsia Society, was created in 1929 and headquartered in

John Hays McLaren

San Francisco. Alice Eastwood, a director and founder of the AFS, was curator of botany at the California Academy of Sciences, which became the official society headquarters in 1944. Local growers created fuchsia hybrids to memorialize the park and city. Victor Reiter, Jr., of the La Rochette Nursery, launched his magenta variety in 1948, naming it *Golden Gate Park*. Earlier, in 1941, he had introduced *San Francisco*, a single salmon pink and orange trailer. Gustave Niederholzer introduced the hybrid *Golden Gate* in 1940, a compact, bushy, red-and-purple single flower.

Most of California's coastal fuchsias, including those in the park, were blighted

by a mite infestation first identified in 1981. Park gardeners tried to keep up by spraying and replanting, but their efforts were futile. Finally, storms decimated the area in January 1995—so much so that park authorities removed the fuchsia garden's sign. Local botanist Peter R. Baye was instrumental in reestablishing the garden the following year, with the Strybing Arboretum Society donating the plants and supporting Baye's work. Also with help from Golden Gate Park gardeners and members of the American Fuchsia Society, the dell was replanted with some 150 plants, including many true species and some hybrids Baye had created to be mite resistant. In the middle of the dell, a brass sundial on top of a square masonry pedestal was placed in 1983.

6 Horseshoe Pits

This out-of-the-way enclave in the northeast corner of the park is little known to park explorers. A marvelous place to sit in the sun or read, it is the home of 16 courts for barnyard golf (a nickname for the out-of-fashion game of horseshoes). The ghostly clang of metal on metal rarely rings now in the pitching courts once tended by the Golden Gate Horseshoe Club.

In 1926, a horseshoe court was approved in the Panhandle, but the sport started in earnest in 1927 when five courts were installed on this hillside, previously a rock quarry. The site was further developed, in 1934, as a Depression-era Works Progress Administration venture; hand-hewn stonework was laid to define the court area. The work included a raised gallery for spectators and a stair lined with large red rustic boulders leading from Conservatory Drive East. The court area was also used for shuffleboard, and picnic tables were located here.

Bas-relief of man throwing horseshoes

Surrounding the courts are two concrete bas-reliefs created on the face of rock formations, one of a horseshoe pitcher and the other of a horse. The artist, Jesse S. "Vet" Anderson, was a cartoonist and caricaturist for the *Detroit Free Press* and later became well known while with the *New York Herald Tribune*. A member of the horseshoe club, he died in 1966. The sculptures had been overgrown and long forgotten but were revealed in 1968 by Youth Corps volunteers. A wooden clubhouse was built in the southeast corner above the courts in 1938, but it burned in the early 1980s.

The hill above the courts rises 384 feet above sea level to what was once a 100,000-gallon water reservoir that doubled as an aquatic garden for irrigating the Panhandle and nearby park areas. The hill has been known by many names: Mt. Lick, Plateau Hill, and Reservoir Hill.

7　Clarke Pillars Gate

This prominent gate frames the Arguello Boulevard entrance to the park at the intersection of Fulton Street, an 1899 extension of the boulevard into the park. The gate was a gift of Philomen Calio Clarke in memory of her late husband, Crawford Washington Clarke, a pioneer Central Valley rancher, cattleman, and banker. Crawford Clarke was one of California's early settlers, having emigrated from New Albany, Ind., in 1850. The Clarke residence was in the prestigious Presidio Terrace enclave, whose gateway is at the opposite end of Arguello Boulevard near the entrance to the Presidio. The Panama–Pacific International Exposition occurred the year of the gate's 1915 dedication, and the boulevard was a direct route from the exposition into the park.

The pillars were designed by the team of Walter D. Bliss and William B. Faville, who presented their proposal to park commissioners on April 23, 1914. Costing $10,000, the gate is crafted of Colusa sandstone and glazed terra-cotta. Brightly colored glazed terra-cotta urns with ram's-head-shaped handles and decorative plaques are distinctive features, as are oval-shaped shields (emblematic of California) toward the top of each pillar. One shield depicts the Great Seal of the State; the other, the Bear. Globes with an encircling band depicting the 12 signs of the zodiac surmount fish-scale–shingled stone roof caps held aloft by eagles. Most of the glazed terra-cotta balusters were removed sometime in the 1960s because of decay, and those areas were filled in with recessed concrete panels.

Terra-cotta, a favored and versatile

fireproof building material of the early 20th century, was available from three regional workshops; these beautifully crafted pieces were probably provided by Gladding, McBean and Company, which was working with Bliss and Faville on several other projects around the period of the gate's construction. The company had also crafted elements for the Spreckels Temple of Music and urns for the Conservatory of Flowers. The company, based in Lincoln, Calif., still creates architectural products used for restoring mostly its own but also other projects.

Bliss and Faville were among a select group of San Francisco architectural firms whose work defined the Bay Area style early in the 20th century. Both attended the Massachusetts Institute of Technology. Other projects of the pair are the brick University Club (1912), situated on Nob Hill; the Ghirardelli Pavilion (for the 1915 Panama–Pacific International Exposition); and the more corporate 1921 Matson Building, facing Market Street.

Clarke Pillars Gate

8   Ghirardelli Card Shelter

Northwest of the Conservatory of Flowers (see site 9) stands an eight-sided contemporary-style open-framework gazebo built of natural wood lattice beams supported by painted steel columns. The column bases are overscaled patinated cast bronze chess pieces, alternately representing a knight and a rook, created by Michel and Pfeffer Iron Works of San Francisco. The woods-surrounded card shelter is furnished with tables and benches, great for picnicking as well as for board-game playing. Outlining the area are embedded dressed granite foundation stones originating from the casino that once stood nearby.

Originally a glassed-in conservatory, the $10,000 card shelter was a gift of Addie Cook Ghirardelli to honor her husband, Domingo Ghirardelli, Jr., who had died the previous year. Ghirardelli had served for almost three decades as president of the San Francisco chocolate company, founded in 1852 by his father, an Italian-born confectioner who had come to California from Lima, Peru, for the Gold Rush. Two-year-old Ghirardelli granddaughter Margery Menefee unveiled the conservatory in the presence of Mayor Angelo Rossi. It was dedicated north of Alvord Lakelet, near the intersection of Haight and Stanyan Streets, on May 18, 1933. It was originally placed near the Old Men's Playground, where tables designated for card playing had been located since 1909. Designed by architects Bliss and Fairweather, successors to Bliss and Faville (see site 7), the elegant conservatory had walls of glass and brick.

In 1937, Addie Ghirardelli sent a letter to the park commission protesting the poor condition of the conservatory and offering to pay for its upkeep. Over time,

Ghirardelli Card Shelter

however, acts of vandalism reduced the shelter to a wreck. That conservatory was removed in 1986 and the current incarnation, the card shelter, adapted from the original. In 1988, parts were recycled in a revised form on the present site for $47,000, through an additional gift to the city by the grandchildren of Domingo and Addie Ghirardelli, together with funds from the San Francisco Open Space Program and the Friends of Recreation and Parks. Ironically, the site selected was near one of the former rustic shelters, known as the Rustic House, that had stood until 1936 and had been used by a splinter group of card players from the original conservatory site.

The original bronze plaque, portraying a bas-relief of Ghirardelli and a Shakespearean sonnet, surfaced in 2000 in a San Francisco scrap metal yard. It had disappeared during demolition of the original conservatory 14 years earlier. The family hopes to restore the plaque to its rightful place among the other surviving parts.

9 Conservatory of Flowers

The appeal of pre-earthquake Victorian San Francisco is alive in the park's eldest structure and crown jewel. As a relic of the Gilded Age—and the oldest public greenhouse in California—the splendid glass house is virtually unchanged in spirit since its assembly in 1878. Covering 12,000 square feet in an E-shaped plan, the 33 tons of flat and formed glass (some 8,000 panes) house a valuable and unique botanical collection, including 700 of the known 1,000 species of high-altitude orchids. The building's important stature has garnered it city, state, and national landmark status.

The Society of California Pioneers fell heir to two crated greenhouses when its wealthy former president, the entrepreneurially minded James Lick, died on October 1, 1876. In turn, the society sold the greenhouses in 1877 to a group of 27 public-spirited and influential men, including tycoons Leland Stanford, Charles Crocker, and Claus Spreckels. Led by former Mayor William Alvord, the group presented the still-crated structures to the park. The state legislature appropriated $40,000 to erect this structure (among other purposes), and Superintendent William Hammond Hall selected a site on what was known as Plateau Mound. Purported to have been constructed for Lick by Hammersmith Works of Dublin, Ireland, the distinguished example of Victorian mass-produced glass and wood was erected by Lord and Burnham of Irvington-on-Hudson, N.Y., supervised by F. A. Lord, for the sum of $2,050. (Lord and Burnham also built the recently restored Enid A. Haupt Conservatory in the New York Botanical Garden.)

Greenhouse history states that the entire framework—glass, wood framing, and the mechanical system—was shipped around Cape Horn. Two pieces of evidence suggest otherwise, however. First, the only known shipping manifest records a boiler and nothing else. Second, during random wood species tests throughout the structure in 1997, some two-thirds of the building was found to be made of redwood, a species grown on the west coast, not on the east coast and certainly not in Ireland. The difference in the other third can probably be traced to the many past restoration efforts.

A fire attributed to a malfunctioning heater substantially damaged the original dome, along with many exotic plants (and a large Brazilian parrot), on January 5, 1883. As part of the reconstruction, architects John Gash and John J. Newsom created a slightly taller but otherwise similar replacement dome in 1884. The $12,000 cost was funded mostly with a donation of $10,000 from one of the structure's earlier benefactors, Charles Crocker. A colored glass window memorializing Crocker's benevolence once looked into the Palm Room but is now lost, possibly as a result of the 1906 earthquake.

Catastrophic damage occurred during the intense winter storms of 1995, when winds reached 103 miles per hour at Angel Island and ripped open portions of the structure to expose the unusual plant collection to the elements. To the disappointment of many tourists, the popular site has been closed since the damage occurred.

Current estimates call for a hefty $19.5 million to execute general repairs, replace wood structural members, and perform a structural upgrade to bring the fragile structure back to long-range use. Close examination of the structure, led by Architectural Resources Group

(preservation consultants), has revealed a lack of appropriate long-term maintenance. Improper installation of waterproofing during past efforts also appears to have contributed to rotting of the wood frame. During the planned (phased) restoration period, the entire structure will probably be disassembled. An estimated 45 percent of the wood will need to be replaced; the remainder will be checked for rot and then treated with rot-resisting chemicals before being reinstalled. Completion of the massive project is scheduled for spring 2003.

Early in the fundraising effort for this project, an unfortunate situation arose. A

Conservatory, 1887, as viewed from the Band Stand

well-intentioned member of the San Francisco Garden Club secured a large grant with the intent of replicating the structure in aluminum and acrylic. Preservationists cried foul for a number of reasons. Complete replacement of the structure with other materials would remove its intrinsic value as a historic landmark and would negate the possibility of using Federal Emergency Management Agency (FEMA) money for the restoration work. This notion went against the ideals of preservation and its benefits in this throwaway-minded society. Happily, the idea perished.

For many years, a sundial graced the center of the Conservatory Valley's central flowerbeds. Park Superintendent John McLaren had created the sundial in 1891 of patterned flowers; it stretched 60 feet in diameter by 24 feet high. In 1939, the Valley was redesigned to its present form. The steep-banked south lawn still demonstrates the 19th-century French-style "carpet bedding" of flowering plants laid out in tightly controlled patterns. Delegates attending the formation of the United Nations in late April of 1945 were treated to a patriotic floral display. Those who went to the park saw floral artwork consisting of red begonias, white alyssum, and blue violas. In 1962, a huge, electrically driven clock with a face made in

plantings was added to the eastern-sloping bank, a $2,500 gift of the watchmakers of Switzerland and retail jewelers of San Francisco.

Large, unglazed terra-cotta urns made by Gladding, McBean and Company sit beside the steps, built in 1918, leading up to the greenhouse; the urns are also placed at entrances to the under-road tunnel. Facing the Conservatory is the 80-foot-long pedestrian tunnel, designed by Edward R. Swain, that opened in January 1891. The south end led through "the Rockery," its pathway lined with rockwork interspersed with exotic plants, to a suspension bridge. The tunnel links Conservatory Valley to the tennis courts. Musicians often use it because of its acoustic qualities.

The form of the Conservatory suggests that its designer took a cue from the elegantly spare 1848 iron-and-glass Palm House, designed by Richard Turner and Decimus Burton, located in London's Royal Botanic Gardens at Kew. The then-emerging interest in raising exotic plants (such as pineapples) out of season depended on the temperature-controlled, light-passing enclosure that came with the new structural technology of spanning large areas with metal. The Palm House was cited at the time as one of the boldest expressions of 19th-century

architecture. Its pure raw beauty inspired the more-decorative Crystal Palace, by Joseph Paxton for the Great Exhibition of 1851, and its New York-bred sister, by architects Carstensen and Gildmeister in 1853. It is curious that the Golden Gate Park Conservatory is primarily a wood structure, yet one whose design seems to imitate the then relatively new industrial technology of repetitive cast iron elements first used in America as early as 1830.

The greenhouse has played a role in a number of feature films, including the otherworldly *Heart and Souls* (Universal Studios, 1993), in which an old-style bus seemed to come *through* the delicate glass-walled greenhouse, accomplished by the alchemy of special effects. Other shots in the movie include what seem to be aerial views of the nighttime-illuminated Conservatory but which are, in fact, shots of a convincingly realistic quarter-scale model shot on its side, with rear-screen projection showing the moving figures behind. Bay Area-bred Clint Eastwood starred here as Inspector Harry Callahan in *Dirty Harry* (Warner Brothers, 1971), and the successful *Getting Even with Dad* (Metro Goldwyn Mayer, 1994) also used the nostalgic glass house as a backdrop.

The venerable greenhouse made news on April 27, 2000, when a clever, offensive strategy was launched to rid its damaged interior of large, flying cockroaches. Geckos, which love to munch on the pesky creatures, were introduced by the Friends of Recreation and Parks.

In 1904, sculptor M. Earl Cummings created the first of his many commissions for Golden Gate Park. Located just outside the main entry to the greenhouse was a drinking fountain with a 5-foot-high stone pedestal topped with a 4-foot-high bronze figure. The piece, "strikingly colored" by patina acids, portrayed an innocent boy teasing a tortoise. The work has disappeared.

*City and County of San Francisco Landmark 50;
State of California Historical Landmark 841;
National Register of Historic Places.*

10 Liberty Tree

The noble giant sequoia *(Sequoia giganteum)* was selected to symbolize the anniversary of the Battle of Lexington. General William Henry Linow Barnes, who gave a brief address during the ceremony, commented that the idea of a liberty tree had been borrowed from the French. The sequoia is one of the unique symbols of the vast scenic wonders of the western United States. The selection of this species probably stemmed from the emerging back-to-nature movement of the time, a reaction to the shortcomings

of the Industrial Age. The movement was sparked by the writings of Ralph Waldo Emerson and Henry David Thoreau, which influenced John Muir toward formation of the Sierra Club. The conservation of lands for public use was part of the concept that people reap moral and social benefits from close contact with nature. This trickled down to the level of city parks, too.

On April 19, 1894, the Sequoia Chapter of the Daughters of the American Revolution planted the tree known as the Liberty Tree during the Midwinter Fair. Squadrons of police, militia, and cadets attended the event. A total of 150 soil contributions from all the important battlefields and heroes' tombs of the Revolutionary War, including earth from the Mt. Vernon graves of George and Martha Washington, were placed at the tree's roots. The Consul of France, M. L. de Lande, delivered a metal box containing earth from the Marquis de Lafayette's grave in the Picpus Cemetery in Paris. As de Lande broke the seal, the band played "La Marseillaise." Over the years, the tree has grown to be enormous with a gnarled trunk.

Native to the western slopes of the southern Sierra Nevada, the giant sequoia can reach 325 feet and has a life span of 2,500 to 3,500 years—second only to the California bristlecone pine.

11 Vanished First Band Stand

One of the earliest structures planned for the park was the band stand, a gingerbread-decorated, hip-roofed wooden shelter built in 1881. The park band used the raised covered platform for Sunday afternoon concerts. Scaled like the small-town bandstands located on most any village green of the day, the eight-sided enclosure had three solid walls to reflect sound out to the surrounding area. It stood at the western end of Conservatory Valley near the Liberty Tree.

12 Dahlia Garden

Plans to build the Dahlia Garden were introduced in 1940 by Interstate Commerce Commission Director Richard T. Eddy and Park Superintendent John McLaren. Their intent was to cultivate dahlia species from all over the world to create an international garden. Located inside the oval of the Conservatory driveway turnaround, the garden is tended by the Dahlia Society of California, whose members nurture its some 1,000 plants into bloom by late August.

Dahlias are a favorite of Bay Area gardeners because they grow easily in the mild northern California climate and come in an assortment of colors, sizes, and forms. Named for the Swedish botanist Andreas Dahl, the first specimens were discovered in the high plains of Mexico and neighboring Guatemala. Spanish explorers had mentioned them when exploiting and developing the Americas and had brought them to Europe in 1789. The dahlia was designated the official flower of the city and county of San Francisco on October 4, 1926.

A portion of city resolution 26244 by the board of supervisors states, "The dahlia partakes essentially of the character of our beloved city, in birth, breeding and habit, for it was originally Mexican, carried thence to Spain, to France and England in turn, being changed in the process from a simple daisy-like wild flower to a cosmopolitan beauty."

12 At the beginning of the dahlia blossoming season in August 1993, a fracas erupted when passionate members of the Dahlia Society erected a door-size informational sign in the Dahlia Garden. Park staff seized the overscaled sign and locked it behind a fenced-in maintenance yard near the garden—much to the dismay of the Dahlia Society. Correspondence flew back and forth, including an eight-page official letter from the city declaring the society's sign inappropriate because of its ungainly size. The general manager of the Recreation and Park Department, Mary Burns, allowed the confiscated sign to be returned to the garden for the balance of the dahlia season, and a more discreet sign was later erected.

13 **Arizona Garden**

The Arizona Garden covers the sun-drenched rise immediately east of the Conservatory, an outdoor extension of the exotic specimens inside. This terraced garden was created in 1894, the year of the Midwinter Fair. The lower part was called the Mexican Garden. Today the beds exhibit many succulent plants and other drought-tolerant species.

An eight-sided landing enclosure once existed partway up the hill in the

Dahlia Garden

Arizona Garden. It consisted of blue-painted wooden lattice walls with highly exaggerated finials topping the support posts. A switchback stairway was known as the Golden Stairs, and a continuous bench lined the perimeter wall of the landing. The bench provided a resting place and a commanding southern view toward the Sharon Building (see site 29) and the Associated Colleges on Mt. Sutro (now the site of the University of California Medical Center and School).

14 James Abram Garfield Monument

Sitting on a prominent berm southeast of the Conservatory of Flowers, this monument, the park's oldest, memorializes the 20th president of the United States. Garfield was tragically shot with two bullets on July 2, 1881, in a Washington, D.C., railroad station by disturbed federal office seeker Charles J. Guiteau. Garfield died on September 19, 1881, at a cottage on

the New Jersey shore. The statue's cornerstone, laid on August 24, 1884, contains a box filled with collectibles, including a copper plate inscribed with the names of those who built the monument, photos, coins, and a Bible. The cenotaph was sculpted in Munich by San Franciscan Frank Happersberger, a native of Dutch Flat, Calif., who also sculpted the giant Pioneer Monument now located next to the city's main library. Columbia, the female symbol of the United States, sits on the base, shrouded and holding a broken sword, symbolizing Garfield's assassination. A bronze plaque shows the president taking the oath of office; it is one of three plaques mounted on the tricolor granite pedestal, made by G. Griffith of Penryn, Calif. Two other plaques flank the sides of the pedestal; both are framed with draped flags and palm fronds topped by an eagle with outstretched wings. The cost for the monument was $28,000; the sculpted parts were cast at the foundry of Charles Lenz in Nürnberg, Germany. The monument was unveiled July 4, 1885.

15 Major General Henry Wager Halleck Monument

Carl H. Conrads's stoic granite sculpture depicts Henry Halleck, general-in-chief of armies of the United States from 1862

Arizona Garden

32

James Abram Garfield Monument

to 1864 during the Civil War. In 1849, as secretary of state, Halleck helped frame the California Constitution. He was responsible for erecting the historic granite Montgomery Block, completed in 1853, where the Financial District's iconic building, the Transamerica Pyramid, now stands. At the time, Halleck boasted that the Montgomery Block was the area's first fireproof structure, a feature proven after it survived the 1906 earthquake and fire. It finally succumbed to developers in the 1960s. The monument, acquired in 1886,

is located along John F. Kennedy Drive, partly hidden in the woods to the northeast of the tennis courts. It was a gift of Halleck's chief-of-staff and best friend, General George W. Cullum. Cullum later married Halleck's widow.

Conrads was born in Germany and emigrated to New York in 1860. He served in the Union Army and moved to Hartford, Conn., in 1866. His sculptural works also appear in New York's Central Park, at West Point, and in Washington, D.C.

16 Baseball Player

While the *"Say Hey" Willie Mays* statue located in front of San Francisco's Pacific Bell Park may be newer, Golden Gate Park had its own version, immortalizing the "boys of summer" long before. Evoking an image of the Great American Pastime, this animated sculpture was presented to the park without ceremony on July 7, 1891, by a friend of the sculptor, Douglas Tilden. It is a tribute to Tilden's energy, industry, and ability. William E. Brown, of the Southern Pacific Railroad, was the donor, although some people have credited James Duval Phelan. The sculpture was purchased in 1891 for $1,700 from Shreve and Company's art rooms, where it was shown in a special exhibit and marked Tilden's first success. After submitting a plaster statue titled *The*

National Game, Tilden had been admitted at the prestigious annual exhibition of the Salon des Artistes Français in Paris in 1889. Following that, the finished bronze was shipped to New York in September 1890, where it was exhibited briefly at the National Academy of Design. The original plaster of the statue was shown in Chicago at the 1893 World's Columbian Exposition. Miniature versions, cast by the same Parisian foundry during 1888–89, have turned up in recent times. The crumbling original base of soft sandstone, designed by John Wright and George

Tilden and his creation

Sanders, fell victim to the elements and was replaced with a copy in granite in 1999, when the figure was also cleaned.

Sculptor Tilden studied in Paris and New York as part of a traveling scholarship and later taught at the Mark Hopkins Institute of Art, a department of the University of California. James Duval Phelan became Tilden's patron when Phelan commissioned the Native Sons Monument, followed by others. Tilden's pupils included notables M. Earl Cummings, Edgar Walter, Ernest Coxhead, and Robert Ingersoll Aitken—all of whom have representative work in the park. Tilden, a native of Chico was known as the Father of California Sculpture and was a master of modeling figures, especially those in motion. He was a deaf-mute from the age of five, a result of having contracted the dreaded, often-fatal childhood disease scarlet fever.

17 Favorite Point

Fowl were raised on the rise southwest of the intersection of John F. Kennedy Drive and Middle Drive East until the 1870s, giving the site its original name: Chicken Point. The summit, once higher than it is today, was quarried away for road bedding material. An 1891 map calls the site Lawn Point. The name "Favorite Point" probably came into fashion later,

with construction of the adjacent suspension bridge.

On March 21, 1916, a cast bronze of Auguste Rodin's *Le Penseur*, or *The Thinker*, was quietly unveiled on the prominent point by the children of its donors, Adolph Bernard Spreckels and Alma de Bretteville Spreckels. The $15,000 gift to the city was fresh from being displayed in the French Pavilion at the Panama–Pacific International Exposition. The original sculpture, unveiled in Paris in 1904, was to be part of a massive composition titled *The Gates of Hell*, inspired by Dante's *Inferno*. The *Examiner* printed an article some months after the San Francisco dedication, trying to convince the public that a more appropriate placement for the piece would be in front of San Francisco's city hall. In 1924, the sculpture was relocated to the courtyard of the Palace of the Legion of Honor (itself a munificent gift to the city by the Spreckels family), where it remains today.

18 Vanished Suspension Bridge

Separating swiftly moving carriages from pedestrian traffic, this 140-foot-long span also became a place from which park patrons could see and, just as importantly, be seen. The cable-suspended bridge was opened on February 28, 1892, connecting what was called Chicken (or Favorite)

Point (see site 17) to the rise just behind the current Tennis Club house, a pathway used to get to the Music Grounds. The span was built for $10,435 by John August Roebling Sons and Company, which had constructed the landmark Brooklyn Bridge and later supplied wire for the cables for the Golden Gate Bridge. The iron bridge consisted of two steel cables, $1\frac{1}{2}$ inches in diameter, suspended from four obelisk-shaped pylons. A colorful paint scheme of two shades of green with carmine red, chrome yellow, and red accents enlivened the rust-prone structure. It was dismantled in July 1928 because of rust due to neglect, a common problem in the sometimes-foggy, salt-laden, moist climate of San Francisco, especially so close to the coast. A subterranean tunnel replaced the bridge soon thereafter.

19 Tennis Courts, William M. Johnson Clubhouse, and Vanished Second Music Stand

The English adopted formal rules for lawn tennis in 1874, and the game has endured ever since. The game's popularity in the park was no exception, where two dirt playing courts were built in 1894. But tennis got its official foothold here on November 28, 1901, with the park's first tournament played on what were, by

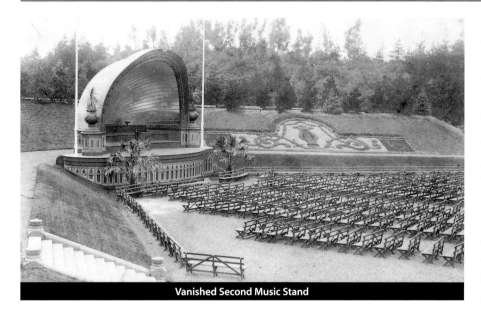
Vanished Second Music Stand

then, eight standard courts (one reserved exclusively for "ladies") and two special courts for children, all initially in clay. At that time, six showers were installed, and soon after the clay on four of the courts was enhanced by oiling. Over time, several more courts were added, and by 1915, 21 courts hedged out the croquet courts. The courts have had an international reputation as a hatching ground for top tennis champions, including H. E. Routh and George Bates.

The current clubhouse dates from 1962 and is named for William M. Johnson, a U.S. representative in the Davis Cup Challenge during 1920–1927 with a record 13 wins and 3 losses. A plaque on the clubhouse was dedicated in 1965 to James Arthur Code, a native San Franciscan and pioneer of Golden Gate Park tennis.

Where tennis today holds sway, music formerly dominated. Some 10,000 San Franciscans attended the dedication on July 4, 1888, of the now-vanished Second Music Stand, a shell-shaped structure that reflected sound. The stand was located where the tennis clubhouse stands today, a design by architects George Washington Percy and Frederick F. Hamilton that cost $2,700 to construct. The shell stood on a curved, raised terrace that created a basin-shaped area to acoustically enclose the area. Decorative embellishments to the shell included a lyre on the top and enormous plant-filled urns flanking the sides. Sloping from the terrace was brightly colored carpet bedding consisting of formal, tightly ordered patterned flower plantings, similar to—but more elaborate than—the floral plaques seen in front of the Conservatory of Flowers. The only physical trace of the music stand today is a concrete stair leading down the slope of the raised terrace. The low, dome-topped newel posts on the terrace once led to the Suspension Bridge (see site 18). With construction of the Spreckels Music Stand, this one was removed to make way for a croquet court before the tennis courts were expanded.

General information: *415/753-7001.*
Reservations: *415/753-7101.*

20 **Sharon Meadow**

This broad, flat expanse of green pastoral turf close to public transportation plays host to many large public concerts and festivals. The lawn and surrounding trees beautifully frame the Sharon Building, seen in the distance, when viewed from McLaren Lodge. Originally, about 1894, this area was named Hammond Valley for surveyor Major Richard Pindell

Do Walk on the Grass

In the 1880s, *Argonaut* newspaper editor Frank Morrison Pixley was appointed to the then-state-controlled park commission; he later rose to president. One day he drove to Golden Gate Park in his suave buckboard, powered by a team of white mules. Newly appointed Superintendent John McLaren joined him on an inspection of the park. As they toured, McLaren pointed out the highlights. At the end of the survey, McLaren asked Pixley if he had any suggestions. The park commissioner volleyed that he had noticed a lot of little signs telling park goers to "keep off the grass." He followed by suggesting that the signs would make a fine bonfire, to which he would gladly light the match. The next day, the deed was done, and to this day, no grassy area in Golden Gate Park is exempt to the public. This simple act defined the park as a pleasure garden for all.

Hammond, Jr., who was president of the park commission and a cousin of Park Superintendent William Hammond Hall.

The low hill north of the Children's Playground, known as Hippie Hill, was a popular sunning spot for the Flower Children of the 1960s and early 1970s. By 1968, the park was besieged by hippies, with their unconventional behavior causing area residents to complain of blatant sexual relations, litter, the smoking of marijuana, dancing in the nude, trampling of plants, and panhandling. Coexisting with the hippies were gangs who robbed park patrons, giving the hippies a bad reputation. Attendees at a Recreation and Park Commission meeting in 1968 described the park as an "evil jungle." Because of financial problems, the police department was helpless to deal with the enormity of the situation. But times change, and today the meadow is a place for drummers to meet on weekend afternoons, drawing curious passersby who stay to listen to the rhythmic beats.

21 Alvord Bridge

The oldest standing bridge in the Park today, Alvord Bridge is nationally known among engineers as the first example of poured-in-place concrete construction using iron reinforcement. Constructed in 1889, it separated foot traffic from carriage and horse traffic. It was the brainchild of engineer Ernest Leslie Ransome, an innovator in reinforced concrete construction who exploited his father's patent for "concrete stone" after arriving in the United States from his native England. Ransome settled in California just after the Civil War and started manufacturing concrete block in 1868. His 1884 innovation of twisted square reinforcing bars is key to the bridge's structural integrity.

Beneath the bridge, a tunnel funnels park patrons from the Haight Street Gate, a subterranean grotto that opens onto lush lawns near the Children's Playground. The seemingly enchanted passageway drips with rustic, natural-seeming, applied concrete stalactites known as *spugne*, influenced by Italian gardens with their cool, shady grottoes. A 1921 publication describes the tunnel as being "russet-hued" and replicating Kentucky's Mammoth Cave.

On July 18, 1970, the benchmark span was designated a National Historic Civil Engineering Landmark by the American Society of Civil Engineers. Metal gates located at each end, added in 1998, are closed at night to thwart vandalism of the delicate concrete icicles.

Ransome later engineered the recently

Alvord Lakelet, about 1901

restored Iris and B. Gerald Cantor Center for Visual Arts at Stanford University.

22 Alvord Lakelet

This small, picturesque, artificial lake was named for William Alvord, a park commission president, mayor of San Francisco, Bank of California president, and city police commissioner, among many other distinguished positions. The lakelet, created in 1882, was improved with a donation by Alvord in 1894. Alvord asked that it be called "The Lakelet," but others insisted that Alvord's name be used. The water feature was restored in 1998 when the entire area adjacent to Stanyan Street was renovated. A bronze frog, the gift of a park supervisor, spouts water in the lake.

23 Page Street Gate

A pair of square granite pillars now marks the intersection at Stanyan Street as a pedestrian entrance. In 1904, however, a gingerbread wood archway here was designated as the only automobile entry into the park. A special park driver's license and conspicuously displayed numbers were required to enter. The road was closed in 1926.

Dew Walk on the Grass

As a reaction in part to the fouled air of the Gilded Age, hygienic movements evolved throughout Victorian society of the late 1890s. Golden Gate Park played its own role. Each morning at 6:30 A.M., hydropathist August Willman led followers of "water therapy" through the grass in the park. The followers would remove their shoes and stockings, a scandalous and undignified exposure in 1898. Believers were there to expose their feet to the purported benefits of the dew-moistened grass near Sharon Meadow and, in later years, near the Garfield statue. The tonic had been popularized by Bavarian priest Sebastian Kneipp in Austria and expanded in 1896 to New York's Central Park and other cities, including San Francisco. A novice began with a 10-minute walk in the cool grass and graduated to half an hour, after which feet were air-dried—not toweled—so as to preserve the beneficial cure. Other complementing Kneipp regimes included moistened towels and various types of baths.

37

24 Haight Street Gate

The third gate to stand on this site at
Stanyan and Haight Streets leads the
visitor to a scenic tour, dipping down and
around Alvord Lakelet, under Alvord
Bridge, and onward to the Sharon
Building. The first formal gateway at this
location, made of wood, was well known
to the park's earliest visitors because it sat
at the terminus of the Haight Street car
line. A grand new gateway, in the form of
granite pillars surrounding benches, was
built in 1904 to commemorate William A.
McCauley with a $2,300 gift from his wife.
That gate was removed in 1979 and the
newest incarnation, made of slate and
cast concrete, completed in 1998.

The first Haight Street entrance

25 Park Police Station

The first mounted park patrol, beginning
in 1883, consisted of one officer: Samuel
M. Thomson. The mounted and foot
patrol park police were originally a
separate entity from the city police,
but that changed with the city charter
reform of 1900. With this came a raise
in salary, new uniforms, and the added
clout of the larger force.

Nestled in a grove of trees, this
recently restored square-plan building,

25 January 4, 1929, saw a skirmish
between the park's feisty superintendent,
John McLaren, and a subcontractor of the
city's Board of Works over McLaren's favorite
theme: a tree. McLaren objected to the tree's
removal to make way for a new paved
entrance to the police station. A tug-of-war
followed between workers of the Eaton and
Smith paving company and McLaren's
pick-and-shovel troops. The tree was uprooted
by the subcontractor but replanted in its
original place by the passionate
superintendent's workers. The tree was again
dug up and the asphalt lain. Once more the
tree was replanted, in a new location, and
the subcontractor's workers retreated,
their obligation fulfilled.

flanked by two wings for stabling 32 horses,
was built of reinforced concrete in 1911
with a $43,000 city appropriation. The
building was known as the Golden Gate
Park District Police Station until March
1932, when a new facility on Fulton Street
was designated with that name. This
building was then renamed the Stanyan
Police Station, Company "F," District 6.
Thought to be unnecessary, the facility
was decommissioned in 1972, but with
public pressure, it was reopened in 1973.

26 Park Emergency Aid Hospital

The mission of the park's former first aid
station was to service the many who
patronize the park as well as the growing
immediate community. The facility was
dedicated on May 15, 1902, as a state-of-
the-art outpost facility (costing $8,488)—
but its operation was delayed, ironically,
by a medical emergency.

Newly hired ambulance driver James
Wynn was unloading supplies for the
facility when one of the horses in his
team became frightened and bolted.
Wynn chased the ambulance, fell while
attempting to climb on, and was run over.
Ironically, he was treated elsewhere, at the
Central Emergency Hospital at city hall.
Driver Wynn died a few days later.

The building ultimately proved a
success, however, as the first publicly

financed medical branch facility in the United States to provide no-cost emergency and general medical care outside of a hospital setting. It was upgraded in 1936 and served its original purpose until 1978, when it became an ambulance station, which it remained until June 1991. The large arched doorway of the south garage was built to house horse-driven vehicles, and the rest of the building housed a medical treatment facility. A gasoline-powered vehicle was purchased in April 1912.

The building's unique style, the work of Newton J. Tharp, merges structured Craftsman design with fluid Art Nouveau details. Beige sandstone clads the front and sides with a replacement multitone terra-cotta tile roof. Elaborate terra-cotta finials once graced the ends of each roof gable. Now requiring seismic upgrading, the structure is currently unused.

Architect Tharp, a native of Petaluma, Calif., was San Francisco city architect just after the 1906 earthquake and fire. He was responsible for firehouses, schools, and the San Francisco General Hospital master plan during his 1 ½-year tenure. Independently, he also designed the base of the Dewey Monument in San Francisco's Union Square in concert with sculptor Robert Ingersoll Aitken; the former Hall of Justice (where the Holiday Inn stands today on Portsmouth Square); Market Street's Grant Building; and many private residences.

City and County of San Francisco Landmark 201.

27 Kezar Stadium and Kezar Pavilion

In December 1910, a teacher from the nearby Polytechnic High School suggested creating a stadium in the natural depression where the park nursery stood. Not until much later did the idea come to fruition.

A monument to another era, when college football was played in leather helmets, the design for the original stadium by Willis Polk was probably inspired by the historic Colosseum in Rome. Park Superintendent John McLaren insisted on one compromise in the stadium's orientation, however. Traditionally, the longest side would have been oriented in the north-to-south direction so that the majority of patrons would not face into the sun. But that layout would have dramatically cut into the park's acreage, so the stadium was oriented east to west. To lessen the impact on the park, the triangular-shaped area between Arguello Boulevard and

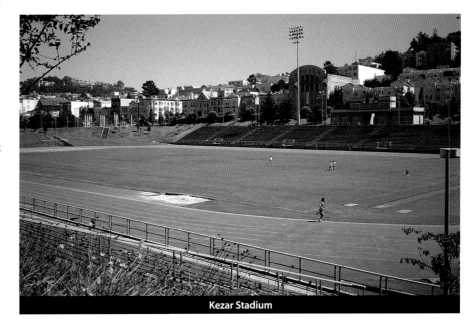

Kezar Stadium

Stanyan Street was acquired from the Market Street Railway Company, enlarging the park's total acreage.

Built by contractor Palmer and McBride with a $100,000 endowment given by Mary A. Kezar in 1922, to honor her pioneer mother and three uncles, Kezar fulfilled the role that an earlier park stadium had never attained (see site 103). The wood-slab bleacher-type seats were noted for their coziness.

Inauguration on May 2, 1925, featured a race between Paavo Nurmi and Willie Ratola, two major track stars of the day, filling all of its 22,000 seats. In 1928, the stadium capacity was enlarged to hold an audience of 59,600. The field served as athletic grounds for Polytechnic High School, across Frederick Street. (The two Art Deco-style gymnasiums that originally flanked the academic building of the school survive.) The stadium also functioned as the San Francisco 49ers' first gridiron home, from 1946 until 1971, when the team moved to Candlestick Park (now 3 Com). The T formation was used here for the first time in a 1940 college game between Stanford and the University of San Francisco, and future President Gerald Ford once played here in a Shriners East–West football game. Because of a lack of parking for the enormous crowds that descended into

the residential neighborhood, the 65-year-old stadium was demolished in April 1989; structural deficiencies added to the stadium's demise.

The current stadium on this site, the new and much smaller capacity "Little Kezar," was inaugurated in 1991, encompassing five acres with open-air seating for 10,000 patrons. The focal point of the field is a huge, freestanding, two-tone stucco triumphal archway to the west, with a design element similar to that of an early scheme for the original stadium. The field also features clusters of tall, freestanding, pink cast-concrete columns at the main entry on Frederick Street. The field, for high school and college football and for league soccer, includes an eight-lane all-weather track oval with an area for field events. It is open for public use as well.

Built to complement the original Kezar Stadium, Kezar Pavilion is an impressively sized cast-in-place concrete gymnasium that seats 4,000 spectators for basketball, tennis, and other court games. The simple design with deep arching roof corbels and multitone clay tile roof was based on the Spanish Mission style. Although intended to open on July 1, 1925, the facility was not completed until 1926. Willis Polk and Co. designed the pavilion with associate architects Masten, Bangs, Hurd and Chace.

28 Carousel

Youngsters of all ages are delighted to be whirled around on Golden Gate Park's multicolored carousel; swans, a stork, zebras, and a host of other exotic animals—even a mermaid—carry them in circles accompanied by boisterous organ music. The vintage 1912 ride was built near Buffalo, N.Y., by the Herschell-Spillman Company. Over time, several West Coast amusement parks owned it; eventually it was installed at the 1939 Golden Gate International Exposition on Treasure Island. After the fair closed, the merry-go-round was purchased in 1941 for the Children's Playground with a $14,000 donation by San Francisco magnate Herbert Fleishhacker. (Fleishhacker had also contributed funds in 1921 toward renovating an earlier carousel that this one replaced.) The new carousel ran regularly until 1977, when safety concerns shut it down.

San Franciscans weren't about to do without their beloved carousel, however. After 6 years of fundraising, 18 skilled craftspeople led by Ruby Newman restored the 62 wooden animals, 4 other riding pieces, and their enclosure. This entailed replacing dry-rotted members and some mechanism parts and installing a used, circa-1930, German-made band

Carousel ca. early 20th century

Carousel today

organ. Painted murals on the carousel's fascia depict some of the park's scenic locations. The final bill of $888,000 was paid by city funds and private donations. On June 30, 1984, the merry-go-round was rededicated.

The carousel enclosure was originally intended to be cagelike and to have a decoratively shingled roof. Ultimately, an 80-foot-diameter open-air enclosure costing $3,500 was constructed. Arthur Page Brown, architect of San Francisco's Ferry Building, had designed it. Completed in 1892, the circular domed building supports 16 Doric-style columns and is constructed entirely of wood. Its inspiration may be the Temple of Vesta in Rome. The original color scheme was white and gold. Stone steps originally created a pedestal for the structure, and a flag once fluttered from a tall pole that adorned the crest; the steps were obliterated when the area was regraded. In 1964, architects Schubart and Friedman commenced work to enclose the carousel with glass as protection against the weather, with a double purpose of seismically reinforcing the building.

The first carousel on this site, opened in 1888, was primitive by comparison. A sea captain named Tyler had created its fixed, gray-painted, wooden horses, and for a time, it was covered by a tent. That carousel was first driven by steam and was converted to electricity about 1915, with a new organ dedicated on May 14, 1916. The original machinery to spin the carousel was in an adjacent building, from which power was transferred to the ride via an underground shaft.

29 Sharon Building and Mary B. Connally Children's Playground

When William Sharon left a legacy in 1886 of $50,000 to the park commission to use as it wished, the members considered several options, including an artificial lake, a new gateway, and ultimately a building and playground for children. Construction of a huge white marble-and-iron memorial gateway, designed by architect John Gash, had commenced in early 1886 near the park lodge, and some wanted Sharon's money to go toward that. Former Park Superintendent William Hammond Hall, then state engineer, swayed the board to use the money for the playground for children, however, and the Sharon trustees agreed. (The partly built gateway was demolished.) Although rain showers occurred on the dedication morning of December 22, 1888, a rainbow arrived in time for the opening address, perhaps leading to the Sharon Building's long popularity.

The building, designed by architects George Washington Percy and Frederick F. Hamilton, is a delightful example of Victorian Romanesque style, highlighted by its picturesque location on a rise in Sharon Meadow. Created as the Children's House, the building was intended as a refuge where children and their parents could have refreshments and play indoors during inclement weather. The Dairy, located in New York's Central Park, is similar in concept. Today the building houses the Sharon Art Studio, a nonprofit organization that offers classes for adults and children, including instruction in glass, ceramics, drawing, painting, and metal arts.

Calamity has struck the building on several occasions. The entire eastern end collapsed in the earthquake of 1906. A major fire occurred years later, on April 3, 1974, gutting much of the interior, and in 1980, another blaze damaged the structure. The final phase of restoration was not completed until 1992.

William Sharon amassed great profits through shrewd, unscrupulous financial maneuvers as head of the Virginia City branch of the powerful Bank of California, through which he gained the title King of the Comstock Lode; he was also known for his poker expertise. Sharon was a U.S. Senator from Nevada

(although often absent from his single term) and a partner in San Francisco's Palace Hotel.

Known as the Sharon Quarters for Children when it opened in 1888, the Mary B. Connally Children's Playground has all sorts of fascinating equipment for climbing, sliding, and swinging. Originally there were also a boys' ball ground and a girls' croquet court. A maypole graced the playground, a throwback to the ancient act of nature worship, an age-old custom to usher in the fertilizing powers of nature. The grounds were rededicated on

29 In some respects, the Sharon Building could just as appropriately be called the Ralston Building after the larger-than-life William "Billy" Chapman Ralston, who reveled in the idea of San Francisco as a great city. Ralston, a gambler and president of the Bank of California, saw the bank's and his own fortunes dwindle to insolvency, which led to his resignation and, within hours, his death. Ralston signed over all of his holdings to partner William Sharon, including the about-to-open 800-room Palace Hotel in San Francisco and his grand country estate in Belmont, leaving the widowed Lizzie Ralston and her children virtually penniless.

March 22, 1978, as a tribute to Connally, who had been park commission secretary for many years. It is interesting to compare the original Sharon bequest of $50,000—enough to build both the playground and the neighboring building—with the $345,960 spent by landscape architects Michael Painter and Associates and contractor Collishaw Corporation to renovate the playground 90 years later.

Sharon Building: City and County of San Francisco Landmark 124. General information (Sharon Art Studio): *415/753-7004.*

30 Foresters Memorial Fountain

This white marble and bronze fountain literally served man and beast: it was designed to quench the thirst of both people and horses. Dedicated on December 4, 1927, it commemorates the 255 Foresters of America in California, members of a benevolent secret society who gave their lives during World War I, the War to End All Wars. Unfortunately, all the cast bronze portions, including the lion's head and flanking basins, are missing.

31 Sarah B. Cooper Memorial

A rainy spring day in 1923 witnessed the dedication of a cast-concrete pool with inlaid bronze lettering dedicated to

Sarah B. Cooper, creator of the first kindergarten of the West and one of the most influential women of her time. Retailer Raphael Weill, owner of the White House department store, had spearheaded a memorial effort in 1912 when he met Cooper's cousin by chance on a steamer trip, but the project lay dormant for several years until the Golden Gate Kindergarten Association accomplished the good deed.

A progressive-minded educator and philanthropist born in Cazenovia, N.Y., in 1834, Cooper had ideas on teaching and the mechanics of learning that were years ahead of her time and made her controversial. The visionary's concept of "preventative charity," as she called it, emphasized that early childhood was the right time to mold a mind. Her kindergarten in San Francisco was the second free kindergarten west of the Rocky Mountains, organized in 1879 through the city's First Congregational Church Bible Class; it became the prototype for kindergartens across the country. Ironically, it stood on Jackson Street in the midst of the infamous Barbary Coast, the city's red light district. Cooper also worked in the women's suffrage movement and had earlier labored to abolish slavery while living in Memphis, Tenn.

The memorial was purposely placed

31 Both Sarah B. Cooper and her 40-year-old daughter, Harriet, died of natural gas poisoning on December 11, 1896, at their vine-covered residence in the Pacific Heights District. The two were found lifeless in their shared bedroom, apparently casualties of Harriet's suicidal tendencies. Sarah Cooper's husband, Halsey F. Cooper, who had been deputy surveyor of the Port of San Francisco, had died of self-poisoning in 1885.

overlooking the Children's Playground by the Golden Gate Kindergarten Association, which Cooper had founded. The subject of the original statue, by native San Franciscan Enid Foster, was a child standing by a pool. A newer figure of carved red sandstone (now in poor shape) depicts a young girl with a squirrel and cat at her feet. Proposed in 1934, the replacement figure was sculpted in 1939 by Works Progress Administration–sponsored artist Jack Moxom, a Canadian by birth who was an architect and a painter. Now neglected, the pool is filled with dirt.

32 Lawn Bowling Clubhouse and Greens

For 100 years, players in traditional white uniforms have aimed their small bowling balls carefully while standing on these perfectly manicured, velvet-looking greens. The sport of lawn bowling began in the park on October 18, 1901, with "bowls" brought from Scotland, the result of a park commission appropriation for construction of a bowling-green. These were the first public lawn bowling-greens in the United States.

The newly organized St. Andrews Society Organization Bowling Club had little trouble getting funds for the greens, because Park Superintendent John McLaren was its vice president. On November 25, 1901, the club was officially renamed the San Francisco Scottish Bowling Club. An official green was laid out in 1902, but the 1906 earthquake heaved the green, and it was further ruined when it became a horse corral for the military housed nearby. The green was restored in April 1907.

On September 17, 1912, the Women's Golden Gate Lawn Bowling Club was formed (women had gained full suffrage rights in California the previous year), and a designated green opened across the street on July 19, 1913. Men and women share the adjacent square, one-story, wooden, Edwardian-style clubhouse, completed in 1916 with a 1971 addition. The third green, built in 1928, hosted a state tournament the following year.

Another name change occurred on January 17, 1931, when the club officially became the San Francisco Lawn Bowling Club, and in 1979, the women's and men's clubs officially merged. The club's membership is now open to all who wish to join in the traditional sport.

City and County of San Francisco Historic Landmark 181.
General Information: *415/487-8787.*

33 Park Nursery and Maintenance Yard

The nursery is the cradle of the park's vegetation, an especially important place during the early years. A small nursery consisting of a greenhouse and seed-propagating hotbeds was established in November 1870 where McLaren Lodge stands today. On November 17, 1870, groundskeeper Patrick J. Owens was appointed to run the greenhouse, among other duties. Initially, fast-growing hardy trees and shrubs were grown to withstand the difficult soil and weather conditions of the park, but more decorative and exotic species followed. Three years later, the nursery was moved to where Kezar Stadium stands today; in 1875, some 60,000 trees were disseminated throughout the pleasure grounds. Plantings of the arid park came largely

from this spot during the nearly 50 years the nursery remained there. With the construction of Kezar Stadium, the nursery was moved again, in 1923, to the area that was part of the Deer Park and Big Rec, its current location on Martin Luther King, Jr., Drive. The facility is not open to the public.

34 National AIDS Memorial Grove

Nestled in the forked intersection of two drives is one of the park's largest renovation projects using a unique public-private partnership. At the valley's focus is the dogwood-surrounded 35-foot-diameter area called the Circle of Friends. Here, names of donors and of people who have died of AIDS are inscribed in concentric circles on paving of golden limestone from Minnesota. Several paths lead the visitor through the valley, which is accessible to the disabled via a ramped path. The dell occasionally reverts to a small lake during winter's wet weather months.

In 1889, the 7-acre barren basin was known as Deer Glen, where four varieties of deer were displayed along with Roosevelt elk, a llama, geese, and, later, a kangaroo and an ostrich. The desolate valley, surrounded by treeless sand dunes, was improved by 1902 with an 1898 bequest of several thousand dollars from

Jose Vicente de Laveaga's estate and designated as de Laveaga Dell. On June 21, 1921, the dell was officially opened for public use, with the intent of cultivating many fern varieties, later combined with rhododendrons and camellias. A dry creek cascade constructed of artificial rocks still exists. A large boulder at the southeast corner entry is the dell's original sign. Its lettering is timeworn, making the boulder difficult to find.

National AIDS Memorial Grove

34 In a city used to controversy, United Airlines was spurned as a potential donor of $5,000 to the National AIDS Memorial Grove in October 1998, because it refused to implement the city's mandated domestic partner benefits and it did not provide bereavement leave.

Benefactor de Laveaga, whose family settled in San Francisco in the 1850s, was a lawyer and financier who owned the enormous Rancho Quien Sabe in San Benito County. He had arrived in California from Mazatlán, Mexico, in 1857. Long overgrown and neglected, the dry lake valley was redeveloped, beginning in September 1991, by volunteers of a nonprofit and public partnership created to honor those who have confronted the dreaded disease AIDS, directly or indirectly. The AIDS Grove was the 1989 brainchild of a talented group of garden designers who, over time, have created a landscape plan with six distinct areas. With the overgrowth removed by 1994, thanks to hundreds of volunteers, planting commenced. The tranquil dell was designated a National Landmark in 1996. Today it supports towering native redwoods, maples, and ferns interspersed with a scattering of boulders, logs, and

benches. Many volunteers have given their time to nurture the grove into a beautiful landscape for everyone's use.

35 Vanished Bear Pit

The most celebrated Park animal ever was a grizzly bear called Monarch, who served as the model for the California state flag emblem. Monarch was a show animal who spent some time at Woodward's Gardens and other resorts before coming to the park. He resided in a special sunken enclosure, the Bear Pit, located at the west end of de Laveaga Dell. Architect Willis Polk designed the enclosure in 1891, and *Examiner* newspaper owner William Randolph Hearst underwrote its construction. Monarch died in 1911, but his stuffed remains now reside not far from the Bear Pit, in the California Academy of Sciences. Sadly, grizzly bears are extinct in California, although Monarch's likeness still graces the flag.

36 Lily Pond

A scenic, dipping path meanders around what was once a quarry, opened in 1871 to supply bedded chert for paving the park's drives and paths. (Chert is a thin, brick red strata of shells and protozoa layered with shale from the lower Jurassic period.) After much of the rock was removed, the area was cultivated in 1902 as Cook's Lake, around which peacocks once strutted and shrilled. Its towering escarpment on the north side provides a picturesque backdrop to the pond, now inhabited by ducks and water lilies.

37 Australian Tree Fern Dell

As if a Tyrannosaurus Rex were about to come out from between the fronds of these prehistoric plants, this area, located southwest of the Conservatory of Flowers and planted with hundreds of exotic, oversize ferns, is also known as Tertiary Valley because it resembles that long-past period of Earth's history. The Victorian popularity of exotic primordial plant specimens is exhibited in the form of the megaleafed Chilean rhubarb *(Gunnera tictoria)*, which shares its time roots with tree ferns, upon entry to the dell from John F. Kennedy Drive.

Exactly when the grove began is unclear, but it was a pet project of Park Superintendent John McLaren's. The tree fern was introduced to the park when a visitor from New Zealand sent McLaren a cigar box of live stalks. Two types of tree ferns were mentioned in the 1890 Park Commission Annual Report. After the close of the 1915 Panama–Pacific International Exposition, many more were likely added, as numerous plants that McLaren had chosen for the

Australian Tree Fern Dell

exposition were later relocated to the park.

These primitive-looking ferns have outsurvived many entire plant species, adapting and evolving while keeping their ancient features. Although four types of tree ferns existed in the dell 20 years ago, only the Tasmanian tree fern *(Dicksonia antarctica)*, a New Zealand native, survives there today. Just east of Mallard Lake is a smaller cluster of another species, the Australian tree fern *(Sphaeropteris cooperi)*.

The Fern Dell serves as a backdrop for *Further Tales of the City* (1982), a volume in

Armistead Maupin's well-known cycle of novels, which began as a serialized column in the *San Francisco Chronicle*.

38 Vanished Canal

The most unusual attraction the park has ever offered was an artificial canal, opened in 1874 north of the present John F. Kennedy Drive, in an area called Casino Hill. The "Canal" was a wood-walled watercourse measuring half a mile in circumference where patrons could experience a six-minute ride and encounter foaming waters, a humble version of the future Pirates of the Caribbean ride in Disneyland. The canal closed in 1896, eclipsed by the larger, but certainly less exciting, Stow Lake.

39 George Washington Elm Tree

Its species native to the East Coast and the Midwest of the United States, the American elm *(Ulmus americana)*, planted at the intersection of Conservatory Drive West and John F. Kennedy Drive, is the offspring of the historic tree that stood on Cambridge Common in Massachusetts. Legend says that future president George Washington took command of the Continental Army on July 3, 1775, under the original tree. Planted in 1932 by the San Francisco Chapter of the Native Society Sons of the American Revolution, the current tree is a replacement cutting from the original. This type of elm can reach a height of 120 feet and an age of 200 years but is prone to Dutch elm disease.

40 Vanished Casino and Rustic Arbors

Brothers Jake and Rheinhart Daeman were well connected with the Big Four railroad titans—Charles Crocker, Mark Hopkins, Collis P. Huntington, and Leland Stanford—through their operation of a rail depot restaurant in Omaha, Nebr. This connection possibly helped the siblings secure the lease for another profit-making venture. Originally constructed as a one-story wooden structure in 1882 for $13,000, just west of and facing the Conservatory of Flowers, the Casino was actually a restaurant that also served liquor. In 1890, the building was moved about 100 feet south to a knoll overlooking John F. Kennedy Drive, rotated to face south, and given a second, veranda-lined story. The face-lift did not alter the restaurant's bad reputation, and it was closed for good after being deemed a bad moral influence on the park. In 1894, the first floor was used briefly as a natural history museum displaying some 15,000 specimens, while the second floor served as offices for the park commissioners and police. The structure

Former casino and one of six rustic arbors

was moved in 1896 to 24th Avenue and Fulton Street, where it was used as a roadhouse. It has since been demolished.

Located in the same area were once Rustic Arbors. The airy shelters were fabricated using natural, bark-covered tree trunks combined with smaller branches to create delightful picturesque images. Four open-sided shelters of varying sizes were built in 1874, in the vicinity of the Conservatory and the McLaren Lodge. In 1902, two more were authorized. The shelters were similar to those constructed in New York City's Central Park, most notably the Cop Cot. Anton Gerster, who had done work in Central Park for park designer Frederick Law Olmsted, designed the bowers. The

last one was torn down sometime in the 1960s after termites caused decay.

41 John McLaren Rhododendron Dell and Statue

San Francisco's mild climate is well suited to rhododendrons, sometimes called the King of Flowers. April and May are prime months to wander this lovely area, with rambling paths once occupied by the giant aviary. The highest point of the garden is Azalea Hill, with a proliferation of species of the rhododendron's smaller relative.

Rhododendrons in the park have a long history. When Director of London's Kew Gardens Joseph Hooker visited San Francisco in the 1880s, he took note of the ideal growing conditions. Later he sent Park Superintendent John McLaren a collection of the plants. In 1892, London suppliers also gave plants to the park. Western America had few endemic rhododendron species (all represented in the park), but by 1893, the collection boasted 44 kinds.

Given all his efforts, it's fitting that this dell honors McLaren, although the rhododendrons he originally planted were on the site of today's Kezar Stadium.

41 The calf of the McLaren statue's right leg is scarred from an act of vandalism. In December 1953, someone unsuccessfully tried to hacksaw the statue down. Just days earlier, an attempt to pry the bronze off its foundation had failed.

Park Commissioner Herbert Fleishhacker and friends spearheaded a fund in 1926 to create a new dell elsewhere, but that didn't happen for several years. On November 4, 1940, the board of supervisors accepted $20,518 collected from public subscription and individual donations to establish the dell to honor "Boss Gardener" McLaren. Ground was finally broken on McLaren's 94th birthday, December 20, 1940, but planting, laid out by Roy L. Hudson, did not commence until 1945, two years after McLaren's death. Formal dedication of the dell occurred on May 20, 1945, when a statue of McLaren, created years earlier, was finally unveiled (despite the fact that McLaren hated statues, calling them "stookies," and had dismissed the tribute years earlier). The planting continued for 10 years. Over time, acreage has been added to the original 21 acres. Winter storms in 1995 toppled many surrounding large old trees that had provided shelter

Rhododendron Dell

for the shade-loving plants, and many have died or are not doing well as a result of the exposure.

With ancient origins in the magnolia family, the rhododendron appears in

41 Botanist Eric Walther worked for 12 years to create the John McLaren rhododendron, a cross between a Cornubia and Falconeri— a fitting tribute to the man who did so much to bring this plant to the West.

Statue of John McLaren with pine cone

41 During the winter of 1921, four owls used the park's Bell Tower as a refuge, muffling the toll of the bell and consequently making workers work overtime.

writings of the Roman naturalist Pliny. An early moniker was rose tree or rose of the Alps. Some 1,000 species of the shrub, which include azaleas, come in a variety of colors and sizes ranging from 2 inches to 80 feet high. Rhododendrons probably originated in Asia, where they grow in the greatest concentrations, but they are found in diverse climates from tropical to tundra.

In the McLaren Statue that the superintendent himself despised, he holds a pinecone and stands directly on the earth, unlike most other statues in the park whose subjects stand on pedestals. Denoting his heritage, a Scottie dog sits at his feet. A park commissioner once said that the statue looks as if "the grand old guy is walking down a grassy slope on his way to give another gardener hell." In earlier times, "Keep Off the Grass" signs were posted on this lawn, another irony, as McLaren had insisted that no such limitations be posted anywhere in the park. Sculpted by M. Earl Cummings circa 1911, the statue was refused years earlier as a gift from Park Commissioner

Adolph Bernard Spreckels to McLaren. One story says that it sat on the sculptor's porch for many years before installation, while another states it was stored at the west side stables in the park.

Two enclosures for birds once stood on the hill just southwest of the Tree Fern Dell, across John F. Kennedy Drive from the intersection of Conservatory Drive West. Because firewood-hungry pioneers had denuded the area of what few trees existed, early San Francisco offered few nesting sites for birds other than the game type; so interest in introducing them to the park was high. The first aviary, built in 1890 for $600, housed only pheasants. The new, much larger, oval-shaped structure was 300-by-165 feet and opened on March 12, 1892. It immediately became home to singing and exotic species, eventually becoming 2,000 in number. Built at a cost of $6,249, the giant birdcage boasted an 11-foot-wide walkway extending through the cage so visitors could be surrounded by the inhabitants. It remained there until the 1930s, when interest in the aviary lulled because of competition from the new Fleishhacker Zoo. The enclosure was later moved to the Children's Playground; eventually it was demolished. Edith Stellman's *Katie of Birdland: An Idyll of the Aviary in Golden Gate Park* (H. S. Crocker, 1917), a delightful

The Renaming of Main Drive

Main Drive was renamed John F. Kennedy Drive on April 2, 1967, the same day an experimental roadway closure let pedestrians and bicyclists have full reign over the asphalt. The pet project of Supervisor Jack Morrison became a Sunday and city holiday event that continues to this day on the one-mile stretch between McLaren Lodge and the intersection of Transverse Drive. Two initiatives on the November 2000 ballot proposed closure on Saturdays, as well. The competing ideas spawned 22 pages of printed discussion in the city's voter information pamphlet but to no avail—neither won a simple majority.

children's book, immortalizes the aviary.

Another vanished building on this hill was the lacy gingerbread, three-story wooden Bell Tower. The bell called park workers to their jobs, tolled out lunchtime, ended the workday, and noted the park's closing. Constructed in 1892, the eight-sided Victorian confection had tapered sides and a cupola. It stood on the ridge south of the Conservatory but was destroyed by a fire of unknown origin during the night of June 8, 1939.

THE MUSIC 2 CONCOURSE

The park's cultural heart is a remnant of the bygone 1894 California Midwinter International Exposition, commonly referred to as the Midwinter Fair. The racetrack-shaped basin, originally called Concert Valley, is a great place to hear the park band play on Sunday afternoons. Other holdovers from the Midwinter Fair include the Japanese Tea Garden, the Roman Gladiator statue, and the Cider Press statue. By 1895, plans were emerging to develop the area into a music concourse featuring a grand peristyle. The oval shape of the basin may have been inspired by the great central basin at the 1893 Columbian Exposition in Chicago.

Wary of the newly created automobile, the park didn't permit horseless carriages on the drive circling the concourse until 1912.

◀ *Spreckels Temple of Music* ▲ *1894 California Midwinter International Exposition*

42 Brayton Gate

This gateway once marked a park road entrance, which was eliminated in 1989. Today it serves as the entrance to a paved area dedicated for the use of athletic skaters. The portal was erected in 1952 with funds from Louise C. Brayton in memory of her father, Albert Paulding Brayton, a California pioneer. He arrived in San Francisco in 1851 and was a noted manufacturer of waterwheels. The semicircular cast stone benches enclosing the park entrance at Sixth Avenue at Fulton Street were perhaps a symbolic plan to recall the waterwheel.

43 Powell Street Railway Shelter

The quaint portal facing Fulton Street at Seventh Avenue served as a major entry and waiting room from 1888 to 1906, a period when steam trains left the roundhouse on California Street, turned onto Sixth Avenue, and terminated at this park entrance. Cable cars later carried visitors to the same entrance. The rough-hewn beam frame building, in-filled with brick, sits on a stone foundation to shelter the benches that line the interior.

44 Brown Gate

The gate at Eighth Avenue and Fulton

Brown Gate

Powell Street Railway Shelter

Street is noted for its magnificent, life-size bronze animals in natural stalking postures. One rough-hewn granite pillar is topped by a lion, the other by a bear. Susanna Brown, a one-time resident of San Francisco, had given $5,000 to create the animals, which were installed in 1908 to honor her late husband, Richard. Sculptor M. Earl Cummings created the feline and ursine figures, while architect Gustave Albert Lansburgh of Lansburgh and Joseph, a firm noted for its movie theater design, designed the stonework.

The entrance road was widened and

the pillars and companion flanking benches moved in 1948 with financial aid from the Beardslee bequest (see site 100). A misleading bronze plaque, installed in 1949, implies that the Beardslee funds paid for the original gate.

45 Chaplain William D. McKinnon Statue

William D. McKinnon taught at Santa Clara University and was chaplain with the First U.S. Volunteer Infantry during the Spanish–American War in the Philippines. This sculpture, created by D. John McQuarrie, was placed in the park on August 21, 1927, 15 years after it was cast at the Louis de Rome Memorial Bronze, Brass and Bell Foundry of Oakland. The donors, the Bay Area Spanish–American War veterans and American Legion Posts, had not liked the outcome of the final bronze, and consequently, the park commission had denied its installation. The statue sat in an Oakland backyard but was finally rescued and redesigned.

Native San Franciscan McQuarrie also created the Bear Flag Monument in Sonoma and the Donner Lake Monument near Interstate Route 80.

46 Robert Burns Memorial

Kilt-clad men and pipers dedicated this gift of the Scottish citizens in San Francisco on February 22, 1908, to remember the Scottish national poet. The piece had been created by sculptor M. Earl Cummings two years earlier and cast by the Louis de Rome Memorial Bronze, Brass and Bell Foundry of Oakland; it was a replica of one in the National Museum in Washington, D.C. A bronze plaque on the granite base includes Burns's poem *To a Mountain Daisy*. The granite base was designed by architects John Bakewell, Jr., and Arthur Brown, Jr., and fabricated by the stoneworks of committee chair John D. McGilvray.

47 Thomas Starr King Statue

Starr King's grandchildren unveiled this bronze on October 26, 1892; it pays homage to the compassionate Unitarian minister who worked in Boston and moved to San Francisco in 1860 for health reasons. Among Starr King's various accomplishments was a book about Yosemite National Park, where a peak is named for him. The statue illustrates his ability as a fiery orator, a key ingredient in his role in aligning California with the Union during the Civil War. (Starr King, who died in San Francisco of diphtheria in 1864, is laid to rest in a sarcophagus, a state-designated landmark, located at the First Unitarian Church on San Francisco's Cathedral Hill.)

The $18,000 piece, fashioned by sculptor Daniel Chester French, stands on a pink Missouri granite pedestal. The bronze work arrived in San Francisco in October 1891 and was originally erected just south of the Rhododendron Dell; the monument was moved to its present position sometime after the winter of 1903. The park commissioners, who considered this to be the best sculpture in the park, felt it required a more conspicuous location at the main entrance to the Concourse.

Thomas Starr King Statue

53

One of America's most important sculptors, French created two American icons: the seated Lincoln statue in the Lincoln Memorial, Washington, D.C., and the Minute Man statue in Concord, Mass. Hailing from Exeter, N.H., French studied in Boston, New York, and Florence, Italy. He executed this huge commission in New York City.

48 Pedestrian Tunnel under John F. Kennedy Drive

Most people don't appreciate the deeply carved Rocklin granite depicting overscaled foliage forms that frames the entries to this elegant bridge. The span arches over a small valley and allows pedestrians to walk safely from Fulton Street, between Ninth and Tenth Avenues, under John F. Kennedy Drive on their way to the Concourse. This finest of several pedestrian tunnels in the park was probably inspired by Frederick Law Olmsted's tunnels in New York's Central Park. The tunnel entries, much of whose design is now buried by encroaching landscaping, are also adorned with symbolic bison heads. These heads hint at the thematic concept for the bridge's design, most of which was never carried out. The design called for statuary combined with fountains flanking the bridge's roadway (where large stone spheres exist today) to represent periods in California's history, a commission intended for sculptor Douglas Tilden. Instead, Tilden's involvement was limited to designing the bison heads set among decorative classic floral motifs.

The subway has cast concrete coffers, by Gray Brothers Artificial Stone Paving Company, which break up echoes and provide a decorative quality to an otherwise plain tunnel. Ernest Coxhead designed the elegant architecture, in 1896; stonework contractor Alexander McLennan carried out the work.

The greenery-surrounded adjacent children's playground, north of the tunnel, was created in 1981 after a pond that had occupied the spot was drained.

49 Francis Scott Key Monument

This "wedding cake" monument has been moved three times—and almost wasn't reerected. Originally dedicated just east of the present tennis courts on the same day in 1888 as the second Music Stand, the 52-foot-high classically styled travertine-and-marble shrine, by sculptor William Wetmore Story, remembers the author of America's national anthem. Francis Scott Key, a lawyer and an amateur lyricist-poet, witnessed the shelling of Fort McHenry on September 13, 1814,

Pedestrian Tunnel under John F. Kennedy Drive

which inspired him to write a poem. Benefactor James Lick was also in Baltimore during the shelling of Fort McHenry, an experience that compelled him to leave a bequest of $60,000 to erect the monument. The bronze portions were cast in Italy and shipped from Genoa around Cape Horn, a 187-day trip aboard the bark *Pietro B.* At the base of the statue are Francis Scott Key's words, originally inscribed in gold leaf.

When more tennis courts were added, the memorial was relocated to the

Francis Scott Key Monument

courtyard of the California Academy of Sciences. When the Academy was expanded in 1967, the work was put into storage. It might have stayed there if not for the help of its fans, most notably passionate park historian Raymond Clary. In 1977, the structure was finally erected in its present location at the east end of the Music Concourse, where the Electric Fountain once stood for the Midwinter Fair. Two time capsules containing memorabilia and records were buried at its base. This installation cost $127,500, with contributions from the Academy, patriotic and historic groups, civic groups, the State Bicentennial Commission, and the state bond issue for beaches and parks.

Multitalented sculptor Story was born in Salem, Mass., and graduated from nearby Harvard University in 1838. He practiced law in Boston for several years but was also interested in poetry. Story worked as an expatriate sculptor in Rome and died in 1895 at Vallombrosa, Italy. His sculptures also include the white marble statue of a reclining King Saul and a bust of a young woman, Dalilah, both in the hands of the Fine Arts Museums of San Francisco.

James Lick, the city's single greatest benefactor, was equally a miser. The grandson of a Revolutionary War veteran, Lick was Pennsylvania Dutch by birth and

early on became a cabinetmaker. Gaunt looking, he lived on a starvation diet and wore tattered clothes. He amassed great amounts of money, however, and also provided funds for the property occupied by the first California Academy of Sciences building on Market Street.

The Koshland San Francisco History Center in the main branch library has an intricately carved three-foot-high wooden model of the monument. German-born Frederick William Heckman created the piece in 1890. It is one of two he created; the other, smaller in scale, is retained by the Heckman family.

City and County of San Francisco Landmark 96.

50 General Ulysses Simpson Grant Sculpture

Several unfortunate events during the creation of this sculpture make its story colorful. Just weeks after Ulysses S. Grant died in 1885, a committee was formed to erect a memorial to the Civil War general and 18th U.S. president, who had spent time in northern California. The desired funding of $500,000 couldn't be raised, however, and what little money was collected sat in a bank account for nine years. When the project finally proceeded, the committee members—Cornelius O'Connor, Theodore Reichert, and

The California Midwinter International Exposition of 1894

After the popular 1893 Columbian Exposition in Chicago, many American cities planned similar expositions to highlight progressive business ideas. Golden Gate Park became the setting for a hastily assembled fair, the first such west of the Mississippi. With a theme of "California: Cornucopia of the World," the Midwinter Fair, as it is commonly called, showcased the salubrious climate and abundance of the state. It opened on January 27, 1894, during the depths of winter.

Michael H. de Young, publisher of the *San Francisco Chronicle* newspaper and the fair's instigator, had been a director and a national commissioner at large for Chicago's Exposition. As president and director general of San Francisco's fair, he hoped the event would help offset the financial Panic of 1893 then in full swing. On July 9, 1893, the fair committee met with park commissioners.

Park Superintendent John McLaren objected to handing over his newly created park to a profit-making venture; he had intended the park to be a haven from just such things. But the highly political and willful de Young got his way. Ground was broken on August 24, 1893, and construction took just five months. The fair was delayed for 26 days, however, because a severe snowstorm delayed rail cars delivering the exhibits from Chicago. (The shrewd recycling of exhibitions saved time and expense.) When the fair opened, 77,248 people attended on the first day, and the seven-month term saw 2,219,150 visitors, a triumph. The fair closed on July 4, 1894.

Known as the Sunset City, the 160-acre exposition site boasted 180 structures representing all of California's counties, 4 other states, the Arizona Territory, and 18 foreign nations. No one architectural style predominated, as it had in Chicago, but rather an eclectic approach echoed California's multicultural population.

Entertainments included a 100-foot-diameter Ferris wheel called the Firth; a spiral ramp climbed by equilibrist Achille Phillion while perched on a ball; the grotesque Dante's Inferno, where fairgoers could experience the torments of hell after entering through the gaping mouth of a huge dragon; and a replica of Hawaii's Kilauea volcano within a cyclorama, a circular building.

The fair forever changed the park; from then on, structures would be built in the pastoral setting. The areas around the park changed as well. Michael de Young owned major parcels south of the park (and some to the north), and the fair was the beginning of the real growth of the adjacent Sunset District.

Isaac Hecht—agreed to shore up the funds to create an appropriate monument. Little did they realize what problems would follow.

Local sculptor Rupert Schmid was recommended for the project in 1894. Schmid, who was well acquainted with the soldier president, had sculpted a bust from life that was installed at Grant's Tomb in New York City. The committee asked Schmid to create a facsimile of the bust as the focal point of the cenotaph. With the project under way, plans were made to dedicate the monument on

Ulysses S. Grant Sculpture

Memorial Day, 1896, and the sculpture was complete by mid-May. It was torn down a few days later, however, a victim of the stonecutters' union and public opinion. To save money, the granite portions had been cut and dressed by convicts at Folsom Prison. The union protested, claiming that the use of prison labor had desecrated Grant's memory. A new base, using materials from the McClennan Quarry in Madera County, was in place by late June.

Complete, the veiled monument awaited dedication, but a new complication arose. Schmid billed the monument committee $560 more than the agreed-upon $8,000 price for the European-cast bronze work. The contract had stated that the bust was to rest upon a shaft of plain green sandstone with laurel wreaths at the base and with the names of battles inscribed on four bronze scrolls. Committee member O'Connor had suggested that a granite base would have a better appearance, however, and committee chair Hecht, who had died in the interim, had agreed to the more elaborate design without the consent of the entire committee. Schmid had overlooked the possible issue of additional cost for a more complicated design, but with Hecht's death, he had no recourse. Finally the work was officially

but unceremoniously accepted by the monument committee and subsequently, on December 9, 1896, by the park commission. If it was dedicated, the date is obscured.

The obelisk-shaped granite pedestal was once draped with a bronze grouping containing a uniform, campaign hat, trench coat, rifle, spear, and sword. One of the four cannonball corner supports has been missing for decades. Shields on the outside corners of the bronze belt note Grant's principal battles.

Schmid was a native of Munich, Germany, where he inherited his talent from his father, a stone carver by trade. Pope Leo XIII and Presidents William McKinley and Grover Cleveland all sat for works by him, and he sculpted the Midwinter Fair's California Fountain, the bas-relief head on the Thomas Larkin Memorial at Cypress Lawn Cemetery, and the Memorial Arch at Stanford University, among many other Bay Area works.

51 Miguel de Cervantes Saavedra Grouping

Official representatives of Spain and South America attended the dedication of this grouping on September 3, 1916. The monument was a donation by two lifelong friends who came to California together in 1860, Eusebius Joseph Molera

and business partner John C. Cebrian, both Spanish-heritage architects. The tribute to the renowned Spanish author includes a bust perched on a cairn, a mound of large rough red boulders, with statues of Cervantes's two well-known fictional characters, Don Quixote and Sancho Panza, gazing upward toward him. Sculptor Joseph "Jo" Jacinto Mora based Cervantes's likeness on a 1600s portrait, the only known portrait done from life. The portrait had suddenly appeared in a garret in Seville, Spain, just three years before the Roman Bronze Works of New

Miguel de Cervantes Saavedra Grouping

York cast the bronzes. The lance currently held by Quixote is a replacement of one lost during the 1995 winter storm season.

Sculptor Mora, a native of Montevideo, Uruguay, moved with his family to Massachusetts and studied art in Boston and New York City. He moved to San Francisco in 1914 and, in 1920, settled in Pebble Beach on the Monterey Peninsula. He also sculpted the panels on the Bohemian Club's exterior and on Father Junipero Serra's sarcophagus at Mission San Carlos in Carmel.

52 Padre Junipero Serra Monument

Standing with outstretched arms, one holding a cross, the sentinel to the Concourse's entrance pays homage to the Spanish missionary and founder of the 21 California Franciscan missions. Mayor James Duval Phelan commissioned the piece and, with the inception of the monument's idea in 1903, designated that the artist should be from California. Park Commissioner Ruben Lloyd suggested that stone for the base should be taken from the spot in Monterey where Serra had first landed in California. The plaster original, artist Douglas Tilden's last work, was created in March 1906 but was unharmed in the earthquake that jolted Tilden's Oakland studio. Shortly

Unveiling Padre Junipero Serra Monument

thereafter, the plaster was sent to Chicago for casting in bronze by the American Foundry Company. Architect Edgar A. Mathews designed the massive granite base. October 9, 1776, the official founding date of the first Mission San Francisco de Asis, better known as Mission Dolores, is inscribed in the statue's base. The Native Sons of the Golden West unveiled the piece on November 17, 1907—not to the tunes of the scheduled amateur band, forbidden to play by union intervention, but to the distant wafting melody from the nearby band shell of "Jolly Fellows" for an unconnected event.

Padre Serra has been a candidate for sainthood since 1934, an effort headed by the Serra Cause group. Despite being a major figure in the founding of California, however, Serra's canonization has been withheld because detractors note cruelties and harm to the Native American population.

53 General John Joseph Pershing Monument

Prominently located on the long axis of the Concourse opposite the music stand, this bronze monument was aptly unveiled

General John Joseph Pershing Monument

53 Brigadier General John Joseph Pershing struck a special note with San Francisco's inhabitants because of a tragedy that occurred soon after he left his post at the city's Presidio, in 1915. In August of that year, Pershing left the Bay Area to command the Eighth Infantry Brigade at Fort Bliss, Tex., to search for the notorious Pancho Villa. Two weeks after he left San Francisco, fire consumed the circa-1885 wood-frame house his family occupied at Fort Winfield Scott. The blaze took the lives of his wife, Frances, and their three young daughters; a son, Warren, survived. Hot coals had accidentally toppled out of an unattended dining room fire grate during the night and ignited the swiftly moving fire. A popular figure in the city's social life, Frances Pershing was the daughter of U.S. Senator Francis Warren. The site of the Pershing's San Francisco home is today the Presidio's focal point, now named Pershing Square.

on the anniversary of Armistice Day for World War I. November 11, 1922, with Pershing in attendance. After the war, Dr. Morris Herzstein had toured Europe's battlefields with Pershing, the war's commander-in-chief of the American Expeditionary Force during the war. Impressed by his escort, Herzstein

decided to commission a monument and consulted with Alfred Gump, of the venerable Gumps store, about who should sculpt the piece. Gump recommended Haig Patigian, who created the bronze in 1921 from photographs. The finely detailed uniformed Black Jack stands, with a symbolically crushed German helmet at his feet, on a pedestal of California silver-colored granite.

Physician Herzstein also donated a large sum to the University of California. Upon his death in 1927, he left the only endowment fund in the park to maintain the Pershing statue and its immediate area.

Paris-trained sculptor Patigian also did two commissions in downtown San Francisco: the bas-relief of Liberty on the Emporio Armani Building pediment on Grant Avenue and artwork in Montgomery Street's original Bank of America building. He created the bust of Herbert Hoover that resides in the White House and the decorative ornamentation once on the facade of the nearby de Young Museum.

54 **Goethe and Schiller Monument**

This gift from the city's German-American community came from an idea hatched at the Midwinter Fair's German Day on June 18, 1894, 100 years after Goethe and Schiller had become close friends. Authors Johann Wolfgang von Goethe

and Johann Christoph Friedrich von Schiller had collaborated on a magazine; in this work, they hold a laurel wreath as a symbol of their unity. Funding came from citizens of German descent in California and from a committee of citizens from Lauchhammer, a town in former Prussian Saxony some 50 miles north of Dresden, where the piece was cast by Lauchhammer Bronze Foundry. The statue is a copy of the original, dedicated in 1857 in Weimar, Germany (where the pair worked and died) by German-born artist Ernst Reitschel. The artist's heirs gave permission for the copy to be made. The larger-than-life bronze, elevated on a pedestal of red Missouri granite, was dedicated on August 11, 1901, in its first location in front of the Asian Museum. The monument was moved to its present location sometime after 1920 at the request of surviving members of the original committee, who felt its "effect impaired" by changes in the valley.

Reitschel sculpted a number of pieces for the University of Leipzig, Dresden Opera House, and Berlin Opera House.

55 **California Academy of Sciences**

Made up of the Museum of Natural History, Steinhart Aquarium, and Morrison Planetarium, the Academy is one of the city's outstanding cultural

Monuments and Statues: Unwanted by the Park's Makers

"The value of a park consists of its being a park, and not a catch-all for almost anything which misguided people may wish up it," according to the first Golden Gate park superintendent, William Hammond Hall. Hall considered the park to be a place to enjoy nature without the trappings of the city, a place that did not include many structures, particularly ones that did not contribute to the true park experience. Yet in an 1873 report to park commissioners about the state of the park, Hall noted, "Some classes of park scenery are fitting settings for works of art, such as statues, monuments, and architectural decoration."

Superintendent John McLaren had even stronger views, firmly believing that statuary would weaken the goal of creating a pastoral setting. Because of his dislike for the structures, McLaren would commonly plant densely around those that did find their way into the park, letting nature envelop them as quickly as possible. McLaren quipped in his Scots brogue, "Aye, then, we'll plant it ott!" after another "stookie," as he referred to them, was placed.

An 1892 *San Francisco Chronicle* account notes, however, that the park was "not very well endowed" as monuments go, a clue that the city's society desired these elements. Former Mayor James Duval Phelan, a proponent of the turn-of-the-century City Beautiful movement and president of the Association for Improvement and Adornment of San Francisco (1904–9), donated several pieces to the city over time and encouraged others to do the same. After McLaren's death, with a new administration in the park, the pieces hidden under his reign were rediscovered. Trees and hedges were trimmed to reveal the artworks, and the press made them known to a generation who hadn't seen them before.

Today the park discourages installation of monuments, suggesting instead that donations be directed toward enhancement of the existing park.

Monuments reflect the culture of Victorian times, when society felt that the presence of physical tributes distinguished bygone individuals and events and honored the courageous accomplishments of civilization. With posterity in mind, the detailed parts, usually cast of bronze, were combined with larger features of natural hard stone. During an era of imperial expansion by the United States, these physical symbols seemed to fulfill the notion of urban beautification. The point of being newly rich during the *fin de siécle* Gilded Age, which lasted roughly from 1880 to 1906, was that wealth be displayed. Mortality and mourning in the Victorian period were reflections of 19th-century spirituality. In an age when high death rates were common and life spans short, memorials seemed to confer longevity as well as be a visible expression of grief. In the context of the new photographic technology of the time, "secure the shadow or the substance fades" was a prevalent attitude.

In some respects, the park is now a repository of remembrances by moneyed individuals or organizations that sought veneration. While most are on the highly visible Music Concourse, others occur all around the park. They range from donations of a select cadre of powerful rich individuals who would not be forgotten, to contributions from first-generation immigrant ethnic groups to denote their growing stature and desire for respect. Still others represent a variety of causes, mostly patriotic. Some simply honor humble citizens for their contributions to society. More subtle monuments abound in the form of roadways, meadows, waterfalls, and the like, all named after their benefactors or an admired person.

Over time, the park's statues have been relocated like pieces on a game board. The Francis Scott Key Monument has been in three different sites. Douglas Tilden and Willis Polk's 1897 Native Sons Monument, currently located downtown at the intersection of Post, Montgomery, and Market Streets, was in the park's Redwood Memorial Grove from 1948 until 1977. The Goethe and Schiller Monument and the Goddess of the Forest, Doré Vase, and Thomas Starr King statues have each been moved to suit the purposes of the times. Some statues— including the original Sarah B. Cooper child statue, the fountain in front of the Conservatory of Flowers, and the marble bust of Ruben H. Lloyd at Lloyd Lake— are gone entirely.

On the cusp of the World War I Armistice in 1918, San Francisco Mayor James Rolph received a letter from a correspondent who signed himself "Patriot" and said that he found the Goethe and Schiller Monument objectionable. The writer stated in the *San Francisco Chronicle* of June 13, 1918, that the statue to "a pair of Huns" should be melted down and recast as a Joan of Arc tribute. Patriotic fervor again reared its head just after the war, on May 8, 1919, when the San Francisco District of the California Federation of Women's Clubs passed a resolution to request that any future monuments added to the park be of "Illustrious Americans."

Some ideas have never made it off the drawing board, but have remained a concept in the artist's head or have been located elsewhere. In 1998, for example, San Francisco Art Commission President Stanlee Gatti proposed that a 24-foot-high stainless steel peace sign be located in the Panhandle. The work of sculptor Tony Labat was intended to commemorate the hippie days of the Haight–Ashbury District, but area residents objected, claiming it would draw a bad element. In 1897, Mayor James Phelan commissioned artist Douglas Tilden to create a monument to explorer Vasco Nuñez de Balboa to be placed at the western end of the park looking out over the Pacific. The model was made but never cast because of the untimely outbreak of the Spanish–American War on April 21, 1898. At other times, simple budgetary problems have prevented perfectly uncontroversial monuments from being built. The Scandinavian Civic League proposed a heroic-size statue of Leif Eriksson in 1936, for example, but nothing came of the Depression-era proposal.

The San Francisco Art Commission has joined forces with the Recreation and Park Department to establish the Adopt-a-Monument Program to raise funds specifically for the restoration and maintenance of the city's monuments.

institutions and a major center of scientific research. The aquarium alone houses 14,000 creatures. One of the Academy's newest attractions, a simulated earthquake, gives visitors a chance to experience the real thing without the risks, while the planetarium features daily sky shows.

This oldest scientific institution west of the Mississippi River was founded in 1853 and incorporated in 1871 with a mission to survey the physical attributes of the West. Charles Darwin was a corresponding fellow of the young organization. Its first home, on Market Street, was destroyed by the catastrophic 1906 earthquake and fire, its salvaged specimens and records temporarily stored at Fort Mason. In a quirk of fate, April 18, 1905, had seen the christening of the research schooner *The Academy*, which sailed on a year-long expedition to the Galápagos Islands. The collections from this expedition became the basis for the new museum after the disastrous loss of the downtown building exactly one year after the ship was launched. The new Academy rose on the former site of the Midwinter Fair's Mechanical Arts Building: its first building, the classically styled North American Hall of Mammals and Birds, was dedicated on September 22, 1916.

Park Commissioner M. Jasper McDonald proposed an aquarium to be located near Ocean Beach in 1901, the basis of which was to be the aquarium tanks from the Mechanical Arts Building; another group insisted that the facility be constructed near Fisherman's Wharf. No funds were available, however. In 1904, Dr. Harry Tevis, the son of mining and banking millionaire Lloyd Tevis (president of both Wells Fargo Express Company and the Southern Pacific Railroad), commissioned architect John Galen Howard to prepare plans for a magnificent aquarium estimated to cost between $3 million and $4 million. The building was to be located in the park, a testament to the Tevis patriarch. Ultimately, nothing materialized from these proposals.

Meanwhile, an editorial printed on April 5, 1910, in the *Chronicle* newspaper recommended reviving the idea that an aquarium be erected in the park. Wealthy banker brothers Ignatz and Sigmund Steinhart each offered the city $20,000 toward its funding. The idea lay dormant until 1916, when voters passed a charter amendment for an annual appropriation of not less than $20,000 from the city to maintain an aquarium.

Ignatz Steinhart's will settled the matter; in 1917, he left an additional $250,000 to fund the building in honor of his deceased brother, stipulating the park

location and naming the Academy of Sciences as steward. The next year, another amendment was passed to cover maintenance, this time designating the park location. Nineteen years after the first discussion of such a facility, on September 29, 1923, the Steinhart Aquarium opened its doors to a throng of 2,500 eager visitors. It featured an atrium swamp enclosed by a bronze seahorse balustrade, which still enthralls visitors. The aquarium was renovated through a public bond measure in 1963.

The unique planetarium projector, assembled from scratch at the Academy, was a beneficial result of World War II. In April 1941, the Optical Repair Shop was established within the Academy to repair naval and army optical and navigation instruments. Special sky-show projectors for planetariums were usually constructed by the German Zeiss Optical Company, but Zeiss had fallen into the Soviet section of Germany after the war. Starting in 1948, members of the University of California faculty, professional astronomers, amateur telescope makers, and the Academy joined forces to create the world-class projector debuted in 1952. The planetarium also served as a light show theater, or lazerium, where laser graphics were projected, accompanied by music. It closed in 2000 after 28 years.

The first three Academy buildings on the park site were designed by architect Lewis Parsons Hobart. (Other local works designed by Hobart include the neo-Gothic Grace Cathedral and the post-earthquake Commercial Building, which replaced the original Academy building on Market Street.) Many additions have been made over time. Following in the footsteps of the de Young Museum, the Academy is currently seeking ways to finance a major overhaul or reconstruction of the facility.

General information: *415/750-7145. Morrison Planetarium: 415/750-7141.* Web site: *calacademy.org.* Hours: *Sept.–June, 10:00 A.M.– 5:00 P.M.; Memorial Day–Labor Day, 9:00 A.M.– 6:00 P.M.* Fee: *Adults, $8.50; children 3 and under, free; children 4–11, $2.00; youth 12–17, students, and seniors, $5.50; first Wed. of the month free.*

56 Robert Emmet Statue

Standing tall in the shadow of the Academy of Sciences is a reminder of the martyred Irish patriot and rebel hanged by the British on September 20, 1803, for his part in the rebellion of 1798. The Robert Emmet statue, a symbol of freedom and human rights, depicts the 25-year-old Emmet making his famous Speech from the Dock during his sentencing. Irish-born artist Gerome Connor created the bronze in 1916, and several hundred citizens attended its dedication on July 20, 1919, a gift of Senator James Duval Phelan. Bureau Brothers Foundry of Philadelphia cast the piece, and architect Charles E. Gottschalk designed the granite pedestal and platform.

57 Ludwig van Beethoven Bust

A thousand people, many music aficionados among them, attended the August 6, 1915, unveiling of the Beethoven monument, which was draped in German and American flags for the occasion. The tribute is a bronze replica attributed to Henry Baerer, whose original stands in Central Park. It was a gift of the Beethoven Maennerchor (Beethoven Men's Choir) of New York City, which performed at the ceremony. The timing coincided with the attendance of the chorus at the National German–American Alliance convention, German–American Week at the Panama–Pacific International Exposition, and a grand concert of Beethoven's works held that evening at the Civic Auditorium. The Henry–Bonnard Bronze Company cast this copy in Mt. Vernon, N.Y.

58 Giuseppe Verdi Monument

The featured attraction at this monument's dedication on March 23, 1914, was coloratura soprano Luisa Tetrazzini.

Adored by San Franciscans, she sang an aria from the composer's *Aida* to an audience of some 20,000. A year and a half in the making, the huge, 52-ton bronze bust of the Italian composer was the creation of sculptor Orazio Grossoni in Milan, where it was cast. Grossoni, who won a gold medal at the 1900 Paris Exhibition, used three life-size allegorical figures against a background of red granite supported by a foundation of gray granite for his tribute to Verdi. The

Giuseppe Verdi Monument

gigantic bust is supported by a bronze belt representing the four muses of Love, Tragedy, Joy, and Sorrow, the fundamental elements said to have inspired the composer. The memorial was a gift of the Italian community of San Francisco, chaired by Ettore Patrizzi, owner and publisher of one of San Francisco's Italian newspapers, *L'Italia*.

59 Shakespeare Garden

Nestled to the west side of the Academy of Sciences, the Shakespeare Garden is a favored place for weddings. The California Blossom and Wild Flower Association established the half-acre intimate formal garden in July 1928 to showcase the plants and trees mentioned in William Shakespeare's plays and sonnets. The Bard had a country dweller's familiarity with plants and included vivid botanical imagery in many of his works, particularly late plays such as *The Winter's Tale* and *A Midsummer Night's Dream*. Some of the original plantings were from seeds from Shakespeare's garden in Stratford-upon-Avon supplied by plant purveyor Sutton and Sons.

The garden includes several special furnishings. An inscribed marble bench recalls Alice Eastwood, director of botany at the nearby California Academy of Sciences, who proposed the garden concept in 1923. Native San Franciscan Harvey Wiley Corbett designed the bench, dedicated on April 23, 1929. On the southeast end of the garden, a classically styled orange brick wall with carved, gray stone details serves as a backdrop for many special occasions. The wall features a bust of Shakespeare flanked by six bronze panels with excerpts from some of the Bard's works that mention plants. Local writing clubs donated the plaques.

Shakespeare Garden

59 A group of women, many of whom belonged to the California State Floral Society and the California Botanical Society, founded the California Blossom and Wild Flower Association in 1923. The mission of the association was to conserve native flora and create an Easter week flower show, which later evolved into the huge landscape and garden show now sponsored by the Friends of Recreation and Parks. Funds from the show are used to repair parks in San Francisco. The association was also responsible for planting the otherwise-barren Alcatraz Island in 1924 with flowers, bushes, and a large variety of trees.

A sundial in memory of Robert Haskell Collier, centered in the garden's brick walkway, was added in 1928.

Placed in a niche of the brick wall is the Shakespeare Bust, one of two copies made from an original stone bust. Sometime before 1623, John Hall, Shakespeare's son-in-law, commissioned artist Garrett Jansen to create a stone likeness for use in the Stratford-upon-Avon Church. Artist George Bullock created the bronze copies in 1814, and this one was installed in January 1928. The second copy resides in Holy Trinity Church in Stratford-upon-Avon. Because

of problems with vandalism, the bust is usually obscured by steel shutters, except during special garden events or by request. The sculpture was a gift of the town of Stratford-upon-Avon.

Over time, the garden fell into disrepair, and a renovation plan was designed by Bonnie Ng of the Department of Public Works. After being closed for a year, the garden was rededicated on June 13, 1991. The many improvements included a sprinkler system, benches, a brick paved walkway, and new plantings. A noted addition is the set of wrought-iron entrance gates made by Eric Clausen of Berkeley. The gates were donated by Steve Silver, creator of the long-running musical review *Beach Blanket Babylon*, in memory of his friend and former city chief-of-protocol Cyril Magnin. With installation of the gates, the original threshold stone inscribed with the names of the garden's original benefactors was relocated to the foot of the Shakespeare Bust. The Friends of Recreation and Parks donated $90,000 of the proceeds from their landscape and garden shows toward the renovation.

60 Big Rec

Big Rec was developed for baseball players at the Midwinter Fair in 1893, perhaps because the Olympic Club was originally located across the street on

Lincoln Way. This broad, flat expanse features two baseball diamonds surrounded by raised areas that serve perfectly for spectators. The east bleachers, designed by Ward and Bolles, were constructed in 1950, and the James J. Nealon Diamond was dedicated in 1960. The west diamond, dedicated on March 27, 1949, honors Charles "Charlie" Henry Graham, catcher, manager, and eventual president of the San Francisco Seals Baseball Club.

61 Strybing Arboretum and Botanical Gardens

Recognized as a world-class living museum of plants, these free public gardens were initially funded by a bequest from Helene Jordan Strybing. Park Superintendent John McLaren had proposed a botanical garden on the site in the 1890s, in cooperation with the State Board of Forestry, with the idea of a facility similar to Harvard University's James Arnold Arboretum in the Jamaica Plain section of Boston. In 1897, conifer species were planted here, and sporadic development occurred. At the closing of the 1915 Panama–Pacific International Exposition, which McLaren had landscaped, some participants of the exposition contributed several international specimens.

Strybing Arboretum and Botanical Gardens

61 A massive, 14-foot-long granite bench dedicated to the memory of the Strybings is placed on the main axis of the Botanical Gardens near the fountain oval. A double staircase cascading around the bench once framed the memorial. Despite a clear description in Strybing's will stipulating "a bronze memorial tablet," the inscription was added to the stone bench in 1951. The request was not granted due to a shortage of metal for the Korean War. Sadly, Robert Tetlow's replanning virtually hid the bench behind the fountain.

A ballot proposition to raise funds for the development of an arboretum in 1900 failed to achieve the required two-thirds majority. After that, the concept lay dormant until Helene Strybing's gift to the city was announced in 1926. This facility was to be one of several memorials to her late husband, Christian M. Strybing, who had died in the 1890s. (Another is a stained-glass altar window depicting the Resurrection, located at St. Matthew's Church on 16th Street.) Some planting began in the mid-1930s, and in November 1937, actual construction began. The Depression-era Works Progress Administration soon augmented the work, managed by its first director,

Eric Walther, using modest sums of money to lay out the initial acreage. The gardens officially opened in May 1940 with eight landscaped acres containing some 2,000 specimens.

In 1960, the Strybing Arboretum Society raised capital funds for an in-house nursery. The first master plan, implemented in the early 1960s by noted Berkeley landscape architect Robert Tetlow, gave the garden its structure, most notably the strong east-to-west axis from the main gate to the Zellerbach Garden in the distance. A Home Demonstration Garden was introduced in collaboration with *Sunset* magazine and the state of California. Edward Williams of Eckbo, Dean and Williams Architects master-planned multiple showcases of materials and structures.

Today the gardens are available for pleasure or for education. Scenic vistas abound in the 55 landscaped acres, including lush gardens, forests, and meadows with some 75,000 kinds of plants from six continents. Many areas focus on geographic collections; others feature specific genera, such as rhododendrons. The exhibits show plants from temperate and subtropical climates across the planet and include a large display of California native plants. The arboretum is also home to San

Francisco's last remaining quail population.

In 1935, architect Lewis Parsons Hobart was appointed to design the Arboretum House. He finished his drawings, but for some reason, that project was never executed. Instead, a 20,000-square-foot Hall of Flowers was dedicated by Mayor George Christopher on August 21, 1960—but only after the mayor had vehemently opposed the structure some four years earlier. Discussion about the building, sometimes raucous, had taken 14 years. In 1956, Mayor Christopher had wanted the available $550,000 fund funneled toward restoration of the crumbling Palace of Fine Arts. Curiously, the entire cost of $548,288 came from a portion of the state's horse-betting revenues allocated to sites with county fair status. The building, now known as the San Francisco County Fair Building, is used as a venue for horticultural groups and is rented for public events. Appleton and Wolfard Architects designed the complex. Plans have been made for alterations and additions.

The Helen Crocker Russell Library of Horticulture is a comfortable place to read, with a wonderful vista of the main lawn from its large windows. The reference library, designed by architect Daniel Warner and underwritten by private donations, was completed in 1972. It contains 18,000 volumes of literature about horticulture and related subjects and has a fine collection of rare books. Rotating displays exhibit botanical prints, watercolors, and other plant-related material. A beautifully crafted stone terrace was added to the northwest side of the structure in 1999 using stones from the ill-fated Santa Maria de Ovila project by Hearst (see site 74) mixed with stone from the demolished Bear Pit. Also housed here is the Strybing Arboretum Society, established in 1955 to support ongoing development of the gardens, maintain their high caliber, and provide a scientific and cultural resource. The society offers many educational and interpretation programs and sponsors sales of unusual plant materials. A cozy bookstore in the arboretum acts as a park information booth from which society-sponsored guided tours depart.

General information: *415/661-1316*. Web site: *www.strybing.org*. Hours: *weekdays 8 A.M.–4:30 P.M.; weekends and holidays: 10 A.M.–5 P.M.*

62 Vanished Pump Works

Without water, the park would wither back to its origins. Water was supplied from the beginning, but at a cost that led the commissioners to seek sources within the park's boundaries. The park commission approved a plan to construct a waterworks in January 1888, to be located near the site of today's reservoir, the lowest part of what is now the California section of Strybing Arboretum. The Bradbury Waterworks, named for well-driller W. B. Bradbury, cost $22,900 to build. The facility was inadequate, mostly because sand clogged the pumps.

A replacement structure to tap a vast, deeper subterranean water supply was finally planned in 1892, just north of the Bradbury site. The additional supply was necessary because Stow Lake was to be filled in the near future. The new facility was completed in June 1893; the cost of $72,414 was, in part, funded with money given by Central Pacific Railroad boss Collis P. Huntington.

The striking building of Spanish Renaissance design was ornamented in a crisscross pattern of Roman brick. Spanish clay roof tiles detailed with terra-cotta trim capped this. The architecture by Arthur Page Brown featured a 115-foot-high minaret-style chimney. A visitors' gallery gave the public access to inspect the building's interior. From there, they could see and hear the roar of the two independent sets of massive, coal-powered, 70-horsepower steam engines that provided the power to pumps that lifted 60,000 gallons of water per hour from underground. San Francisco's Union

A Bequest of Treasures?
The Strybing Stones and Coins

Helene Strybing died on Christmas Eve day in 1926. She was the widow of Christian Strybing, variously thought to be a silk merchant, lumber magnate, or owner of a diamond mine in South Africa. Helene left a legacy of $100,000 for the construction of gardens in the park and an additional endowment of $150,000 in 1939 with the death of her last close relative. The legacy included a cache of six unflawed, brilliantly green, intricately cut African emeralds, totaling 16 carats, and a handful of old coins.

In 1941, Mayor Angelo Rossi requested an appraisal of the baubles, possibly to cash the gems in to buy war bonds. But they were found to be paste—a very good grade of glass. No one doubted that the wealthy widow could have afforded the real thing, and judging from her will, she seemed to have thought the impostors were real. The coins, too, were worth a mere $49. For decades, the items were shuttled around to various agencies, forgotten, rediscovered, and reappraised. They have taken on a historic value all their own and currently reside on display in the Koshland San Francisco History Center of the main public library. Little is known about the enigmatic Strybings, let alone about this conundrum.

Iron Works, world-famed builders of battleships and mining machinery, fabricated the engines. The pump station supplied water to the reservoir on Strawberry Hill for gravity feed to the park's irrigation system.

The picturesque facility was fatally damaged by a quick-moving blaze and explosion on June 30, 1916. A much smaller, innocuous concrete building containing electric pumps to extract water from the wells now occupies the site.

63 Spreckels Temple of Music

Audiences love the free Sunday afternoon concerts performed by the Golden Gate Park Band, a park institution since the 1880s. The band has an impressive backdrop, the third bandstand to grace the park. In 1895, because of the growing patronage, discussions started about a larger stand to be located on the Midwinter Fair's site of the allegorical Statuary Fountain.

The classically styled grand band shell is similar to another such structure built in Bellingham, Wash., also designed by Reid Brothers architects. Styled in the Italian Renaissance tradition, the acoustically reflective coffered shell stands 70 feet high and is faced with Colusa sandstone. German-born Claus "The Sugar King" Spreckels gave

$75,000 toward the majestic building's $78,810 cost, convinced by his son Adolph Bernard, president of the park commission, to make the donation.

The band shell was dedicated on September 9, 1900, with an audience of some 75,000 filling the valley. General William Henry Linow Barnes noted that it was "an architectural poem set to music." The major earthquake six years later did considerable damage, but the structure was repaired. Time and the 1989 Loma Prieta quake took a furthur toll, and the city undertook a $2 million restoration and seismic upgrading, completed in 1994.

64 The Music Concourse and Fountains

A grove of lichen- and moss-encrusted trees covers the sunken amphitheater, creating a subterranean world with glimpses to four surrounding splashing fountains and a music shell. The trees are mostly London plane (*Platanus* x *acerifolia*) and are pollarded, or trimmed using an annual severe pruning technique that results in a uniform, dome-shaped crown. The structure can accommodate an audience of some 20,000 to enjoy the music *alfresco* under the canopy.

Created for the Midwinter Fair's Grand Court of Honor, the form was

sculpted from the dunes by many men using horse-drawn sleds to create the symmetrical, oval-shaped landscape of what was to become "Concert Valley." The focus of the sunken concourse is a large, low-curbed, circular fountain with a sculpture of a rampant tiger defending itself against an entwined serpent, all amid gently spouting water. Architect Herbert A. Schmidt designed the cast artificial stone pool, while M. Earl Cummings sculpted the statue of the same material. Cummings had hoped the statue could be bronze, but budget constraints affected that idea.

Corinne Rideout, widow of banker Norman D. Rideout, donated $10,000 of her husband's $100,000 estate toward the Rideout Fountain installed in 1924. Norman Rideout, who had died in 1907, had arrived in the Sacramento Valley in 1851 from Maine and started a bank in Oroville, followed by five more in the Valley. After his death, his widow sold the chain of banks to Amadeo P. Giannini of the Bank of Italy, which later became the titan Bank of America.

Two smaller circular fountains that flank the Rideout Fountain, contained by granite coping, were completed in 1914. These Page Fountains were a gift of the widow of Charles Page, in memory of her husband, a prominent admiralty attorney.

Born in Valparaíso, Chile, Page was president of the Title and Trust Insurance Company and a director of the Fireman's Fund Insurance Company.

The last of the four fountains at this site, an elegant double-tier fountain made of cast artificial stone, rises off the south side of the Music Concourse adjacent to the entrance of the California Academy of Sciences. Surrounded by a pair of classic sweeping staircases, this fountain is a tribute to philanthropist Phoebe Apperson Hearst. Donations toward the final cost of $11,342 were sought by public subscription, starting in 1923, spearheaded by Hearst's many influential friends. During the September 16, 1926, Park Commission Board meeting, Corinne S. Koshland of the Levi Strauss family presented the fountain's design to the park board, which unanimously approved it. The Phoebe Apperson Hearst Memorial Association intended the fountain to be placed in a prominent location, such as in front of the Civic Center's main library, but that was not to be. With Phoebe Hearst's keen interest in education, especially for children, the location adjacent to the California Academy of Sciences proved prophetic. Architects John Bakewell, Jr., and Arthur Brown, Jr. (who also designed the Civic Center's magnificent city hall), designed

the memorial, which was executed by Travertex Stone Corporation.

A far-sighted philanthropist with many causes, Phoebe Apperson Hearst was an especially great benefactor to education, artists, and architects. The widow of politically ambitious mining mogul George Hearst, she was the first female regent of the University of California, and her many gifts had a great impact on the Berkeley campus. She was cofounder of the Parent Teacher Association and underwrote schools in Washington, D.C., as well.

65 Lion Statue

Many admiring hands have stroked the robust seated figure of the King of Beasts, wearing its patined bronze down a bit. This smaller-than-life cat was created by artist Ronald Hinton Perry in 1898 and was a gift, in 1906, by the venerable San Francisco jeweler Shreve and Company. The sculpture survived a fire in Shreve's showroom caused by the 1906 earthquake. The lion is mounted on a contrasting natural red stone boulder donated by John D. McGilvray.

Both a portrait painter and a sculptor, Perry was born in New York in 1870 and was later schooled at the famed École des Beaux-Arts in Paris. His works include figures of massive lions perched on the

Lion Statue

Connecticut Avenue Bridge in Washington, D.C., and relief panels in the recently restored New Amsterdam Theater in New York.

66 Doré Vase

This unique sculpture invites visitors to survey its lush surface, behind which lie several stories. The monumental piece, 22 feet in circumference, is titled *The Story of the Vine (Poème de la Vigne)*. The 6,000-pound cast bronze vessel has

58 separately formed animated figures, entwined with grapevines, visually narrating the story of winemaking. A close look at the base reveals cupids battling growth-destroying insects, as cupids above squeeze the abundant fruit of its juice. Larger playful figures feature Bacchus (the god of wine), Silenus (the drunken attendant and nurse to Bacchus), the Goddess Diana (lover of woods and wild things), satyrs (attendants to Bacchus), and bacchantes (priestesses of

Doré Vase

Bacchus). Although touted as an original, some believe the vase might be a copy.

Frenchman Paul Gustave Doré created the 11-foot-high vessel in 1877–78. When the French Thiebaut Brothers Foundry finished casting the piece, Doré's finances were in the red, and with his death five years later, the bill was still unpaid. In an attempt to retrieve its money, the foundry sent the extravagant piece to the World's Columbian Exposition of 1893 in Chicago, where it was exhibited for a viewing fee. There, San Franciscan Michael de Young, a director and a national commissioner at large to the fair, saw it. After the Chicago venue closed, the vase was shipped to California, an apt move with California wine already touted as the best in the United States. When the Midwinter Fair closed, de Young desired to keep the piece for the Memorial Museum he was about to launch. The asking price was 80,000 francs for the casting, storage, and shipment, but in a shrewd business maneuver, de Young paid the foundry only 50,000 francs ($11,000) in cash. (The vase was valued in 1917 at $225,000.) The vase has been moved over the years but today sits approximately in its original place, where it was returned just in time to commemorate the 100th anniversary of the Midwinter Fair.

67 The Sphinxes

This pair of crouched Egyptian mythical figures by sculptor Arthur Putnam guards a walkway seemingly to nowhere—but this was once the pathway to the Egyptian-style Fine Arts Building for the 1894 Midwinter Fair. These figures replace the original ones, which disappeared sometime after the 1906 earthquake. Stories abound about the material and fate of the originals. Some say they were granite, and others say they were bronze that was melted down. Another memory is that one was stolen and the other destroyed. In any event, the current concrete pieces, similar in concept to the original ones, were created in 1903 and installed in 1928.

Putnam is known for his animal sculptures; he also sculpted (with Leo Lentelli) Market Street's decorative streetlight bases.

68 Apple Cider Press Statue

Over the years, many people have assumed that this remnant of the Midwinter Fair represents a taut-muscled nude crushing wine grapes. But closer inspection reveals that the fruits are apples and that this was once a drinking fountain with a drinking cup attached by a chain as part of its subject matter.

Apple Cider Press Statue

Sculptor Thomas Shields–Clarke of Pittsburgh, Penn., executed the piece in 1892; Jaboeuf and Bezout in Paris cast it. Michael de Young and the California Midwinter Fair Commission purchased the piece from the French Commission in 1894. The catch bucket is a copy of the original, which was stolen in 1989.

69 Sundial

This charming yet functional piece still tells solar time and celebrates three early navigators of California's coast. The three-quarter sphere with a bas-relief map of the Americas commemorates Portuguese Juan Rodriguez de Cabrillo, who explored the bay of San Diego on September 28, 1542; Spaniard Fortuno Ximenes, the first European to explore the Baja Peninsula in 1534; and Englishman Sir Francis Drake, who on June 17, 1579, sailed the bay later named for him at Pt. Reyes, Marin County. Sitting on top of a fluted white granite column is a partial globe with a flat face oriented toward the sun. The globe is perched on the back of a sea turtle, based on the Native American myth in which the land is mounted on the back of a turtle's shell, and earthquakes are caused when the turtle moves. Sculptor M. Earl Cummings took two years to complete the monument. A present from the National Society of Colonial Dames of America in California, it was unveiled on a sunny Columbus Day, October 12, 1907.

70 Roman Gladiator Sculpture

This piece, of a lunging soldier holding his sword aloft, is the work of 76-year-old sculptor Guillaume Geefs. The bronze, created in 1881, was a symbolic cornerstone to launch construction on August 24, 1893, for the 1894 California Midwinter Fair. An eager crowd of 60,000 spectators witnessed the kickoff event, with hopes that the fair would bring badly needed work to the area during a recession. But the sculpture didn't help them; it was cast

Roman Gladiator Statue

by Cie des Bronzes of Brussels, Belgium, and the base was cut by convicts at Folsom Prison, bringing complaints from the local stonecutters' union in a precursor to the debate over the base of the Ulysses S. Grant pedestal nearby.

71 M. H. de Young Memorial Museum and Asian Art Museum

Sculptor Douglas Tilden advocated a public museum in the park with his article "Art, and What San Francisco Should Do About Her" in the May 1892 issue of *Overland Monthly*. That same year,

World War I Propaganda Movie

As the dark clouds of World War I began to part in 1918 Europe, prominent citizen Michael de Young, proprietor of the *San Francisco Chronicle*, sponsored a film to boost the morale of battle-weary troops on the French front line. The visual postcard, produced by Thomas Harper Ince, showed wives, children, mothers, sweethearts, and families sending greetings from home. De Young may have chosen Ince because he directed a 1914 feature film, *Civilization*, which pled for pacifism with its antiwar theme. The organizers had suggested that the women and girls wear the same clothes they wore on the day they bid good-bye to their soldiers. The film also portrayed a drive down Market Street and, in another sequence, a ride around the park. The concept was to illustrate a familiar Sunday afternoon in San Francisco. A throng of 150,000 people, some from distant parts of California, congregated in the Big Rec Ball Field near Eighth Avenue and Lincoln Way on the sunny Sunday afternoon of October 6, 1918. The rally started with a group picture in Big Rec; then military bands escorted the masses, including organizations, societies, and unions, to the drive in front of the de Young Museum. All together, 12,000 feet of film were shot as the parade marched.

the philanthropic and energetic Phoebe Apperson Hearst suggested a public museum in Golden Gate Park, whose genesis would be her art collections (then stored in warehouses in New York, Washington, D.C., and San Francisco). Her wealthy husband, Senator George Hearst, had died in 1891, and Phoebe Hearst was parceling money out to "instructive" institutions. She had intended to give $1 million for a museum and an equal amount as an endowment for maintenance. Instead, in 1896, she funded a master plan for Berkeley's University of California campus. Shortly thereafter, the other newspaper-publishing family in town, the de Youngs, took up the cause of a museum in the park.

The current city museum system started with the exotic, Egyptian-style Fine and Decorative Arts Building, recycled from the California Midwinter International Exposition. After the fair closed, profits financed conversion of the building and the adjacent Royal Bavarian Pavilion to a permanent museum, the Midwinter Memorial Museum, inaugurated on March 21, 1895, with a diverse collection of some 6,000 objects. The Bavarian Pavilion, whose contents were brought from Chicago's Columbian Exhibition at a cost of some $81,000, consisted of four reproduction rooms

copied from mad King Ludwig's Royal Pavilion in Munich. The museum's original collections were given primarily by Michael (M. H.) de Young; an eclectic mix of donations from San Francisco's citizens has since augmented the collection. The building, graced with representations of Hathor the Cow Goddess, was designed by Charles C. McDougall. With the museum's popularity, an annex was later built. Having outgrown their use, the buildings were condemned and destroyed in 1929.

Construction of a new museum building began when the east wing's cornerstone was laid on April 15, 1917, on what was part of the former site of the Midwinter Fair's Horticultural and Agricultural Building. Architect Louis Christian Mullgardt was commissioned by de Young, who insisted that the elaborate 16th-century Spanish Renaissance Baroque style be used. Mullgardt, on the architectural board of the Panama–Pacific International Exposition, had used that same style in his design for the well-received Court of the Ages at that exposition. Combining luxury and wealth with a vague allusion to the state's Spanish heritage, Mullgardt's concoction drew from many sources. The encrusted ornamental confection, in a color scheme of pink-and-white, originally featured symbols and allegorical figures depicting California, themselves sculpted by Haig Patigian and Leo Lentelli (who also sculpted the bases for Market Street's light standards). The center section was dedicated on January 2, 1921, and the museum's name was changed to the M. H. de Young Memorial Museum. The iconic tower looms 134 feet high over the main entry; its construction was funded by Mary A. Burke. The west wing was added in 1926, completing the facade that architect Mullgardt had envisioned 10 years earlier.

The steel and reinforced concrete complex was built by Lindgren Company, forerunner to the venerable Swinerton and Walberg, which also built the Fairmont Hotel. In 1949, City Architect Dodge A. Riedy dramatically changed the appearance of the building when he stripped the three-dimensional decorative ornaments at the advice of architect Arthur Brown, Jr. The removal of the ornaments seemed to echo the modernizing of many older-style structures at the time, but it had a functional basis as well. The concrete ornamentation had started peeling off the exterior in 1931, because ongoing neglect during the Depression years had led to rusting of the iron reinforcing rods, and a temporary wooden shed was

needed around the main entry to protect unwary patrons from potential injury.

After the 1989 Loma Prieta earthquake, 14 gray-painted steel buttresses were added in 1994 as seismic bracing, just in time for the museum's centennial. This was only a temporary measure, however. Too small for its own eclectic but superb collection (especially strong in U.S., African, and Oceanic art and in the art of the Americas) and too unsafe to meet special insurance requirements for traveling exhibits, the de Young building requires replacement.

With the dawn of the 21st century, a new chapter began in the museum's history. In 1997, museum trustees voted overwhelmingly to pursue a new museum location downtown; they did not feel it was "fiscally responsible" to continue in the park. Two bond measures to rebuild the museum with public funds were proposed but fell short of approval. Ultimately, the building will be rebuilt on the same site with private funding. Swiss architects Jacques Herzog and Pierre de Meuron, who also designed the Tate Modern's new building in London, have been commissioned to design the structure, slated to open in 2006. The quantum-move-forward design for the project is minimalist in style, incorporating 280,000 square feet, with

three stories over a below-grade-level structure surmounted by a 180-foot-tall tower, a vestige of the original tower. With a projected price of $135 million, the new facility will double the existing floor area but take up less space. When the design was unveiled in June 1999, reactions were mixed; historicists voiced some concern about the sleekness of an "Aircraft Carrier de Young" in a Victorian park. Adjustments to the design have been made, and construction is slated to start in late 2001 after a series of bureaucratic and public reviews. The de Young closed in December 2000 for reconstruction.

Under the same roof as the de Young Museum is the independent Asian Art Museum of San Francisco, the largest collection of Asian art and artifacts in the Western world. Completed in 1966 with a gift from Avery Brundage, the museum comprises more than 12,000 objects representing some 40 countries of Asian culture. Architect Gardner Dailey, a veteran of architect Julia Morgan's office, designed the wing that replaced the 1921 west extension. The Asian Museum will close its doors in fall 2001 to move to its new quarters in the Civic Center's recycled former main library, asserting its independence as a major collection, in fall 2002.

Outside of the museums, the four

71 Four uninsured Dutch paintings were stolen from the de Young Museum on Christmas Eve, 1978. One, Rembrandt's *Portrait of a Rabbi,* was estimated to be worth $1 million; the other three totaled some $57,000. A similar attempt on the Rabbi had been made during the previous August but had been thwarted. Authorities assume that the same party was involved in the Christmas Eve heist. The FBI was brought into the investigation, but the thief has never been caught.

Much to the surprise of the museum, some of the treasures were recovered 21 years after their theft. An unknown person dropped off three of the paintings, including the Rabbi, at New York's Doyle Gallery on November 2, 1999.

corners of the outdoor Oakes Garden pool are anchored with fantastic sculptures depicting larger-than-life-size trios of cupids. Originally part of the Midwinter Fair, these bronze replicas were cast by Thiebault–Freres of Paris from the originals by French sculptor Francois Lespongola. They were initially placed in front of the first museum building and were later mounted on pedestals in front of the Temple of Music, where large planters now stand. They

were moved to their present location in 1955. The originals once stood around the Parterre d'Eau at the Palace of Versailles.

Location: *75 Hagiwara Tea Garden Way.* General information (Asian Art Museum): *415/379-8800.* Web site (de Young Museum): *famsf.org/deYoung.* Web site (Asian Art Museum): *asianart.org.* Hours: *Tues.–Sun., 9:30 A.M.–5:00 P.M.; first Wed. of the month, 9:30 A.M.–8:45 P.M.* Fee: *Adults, $7.00; children 12 and under, free; youth 12–17, $4.00; seniors, $5.00; first Wed. and Sat. morning of the month, free.* Accessibility information: *415/750-7645.*

72 **Pool of Enchantment**

Visitors are indeed enchanted to find turtles basking on rocks in this naturalistic pool that graces the ramped front entry to the de Young Museum. In the middle of the pool is a landscaped island where stands a yard-high bronze depiction of a Native American boy. The figure, sculpted by M. Earl Cummings and dedicated on September 29, 1917, plays his pipes to two California mountain lions. Architect Herbert A. Schmidt designed the formal pool; Schmidt also designed the German Savings and Loan Society Building in San Francisco's Mission District.

Donor Maria Becker, widow of banker Bernard Adolph Becker, had another idea

for the use of her $42,000 bequest; she intended to erect a colonnaded observatory on top of Strawberry Hill to replace the two-story Sweeney Observatory toppled by the 1906 earthquake. The park commission rejected the design proposal at its April 5, 1917, meeting, and the pool and sculptures were the compromise.

This popular pool is slated to be moved to the east end of the museum site after the de Young Museum is rebuilt.

Pool of Enchantment

73 Japanese Tea Garden

One of San Francisco's most visited attractions is the Japanese Tea Garden. The exotic landscape looks like a stage set with its undulating, moss-covered hill punctuated with beautifully placed sculpture and landscaping. The best time to visit is in April, when the delicate cherry blossoms are at their peak.

There are two different stories about development of this oldest Japanese-style garden in the United States. Years after the garden's centennial, it is difficult to know which is correct. Some people give more credit to George Turner Marsh, while others feel Makoto Hagiwara was the primary founder. Park Superintendent John McLaren stated that Hagiwara actually built the original garden and its structures.

A relic of the 1894 California Midwinter Fair, the garden originally occupied one acre within the Japanese Village exhibit. Its creation was perhaps inspired by a similar exhibit at the 1893 Columbian Exposition in Chicago, although San Francisco's version was much more authentic and elaborate. According to one story, a wealthy Japanese landscape gardener, Makoto Hagiwara, son of an Osaka landholder and industrialist, designed and constructed the landscape as a Japanese rural-style garden. In 1895,

Japanese Tea Garden

Hagiwara was appointed as the official caretaker of his creation. The garden was enlarged in 1902, with another addition in 1916 consisting of the area west of the teahouse. That expansion included a pagoda, gateways, and other art removed from the Panama–Pacific International Exposition after that fair closed. The Hagiwara family resided in a 17-room house that stood northeast of the teahouse in the Sunken Garden area. Hagiwara supported newly arrived Japanese immigrants, who exchanged their services as gardeners for free board while they sought American citizenship, and expanded the garden to five acres before his death in 1925. Later, his son-in-law, Goro Tozawa Hagiwara, managed the gardens until his demise in 1937, after which Goro Hagiwara's wife Takano took over with the help of her children.

Tragically, after 48 years of U.S. residency, the Hagiwara family was evicted from the garden it had worked so hard to cultivate, victims of the hysteria accompanying the outbreak of World War II. The War Department's Relocation Directive forced the family out on May 20, 1942, sending Hagiwara descendants to an internment camp in Utah and transferring the garden to the city. The garden was renamed the Oriental Tea Garden, and the Hagiwara house was demolished.

73 A seminal act took place when that famous Chinese restaurant cliché, the fortune cookie, was created and first served—not in China, but in the Japanese Tea Garden—in 1914.

During his many trips to Asia, Hagiwara had assembled a large collection of bonsai trees and art objects that he had displayed in the garden. Just before internment, his descendants removed the collection to the Marin County property of a family friend and designer of Japanese gardens, Samuel Newsom. After the Hagiwara family's release, Takano Hagiwara requested in July 1950 that Newsom liquidate many of the family treasures. The specimens were sold to Dr. Hugh M. Fraser, who maintained them at his Oakland home. (With the death of the doctor, and later of his wife, the collection was returned to the park, with some additions, on April 26, 1966, with design advice from Newsom.) After a letter-writing campaign, the word "Japanese" was reinstated to the name of the garden on October 23, 1952.

A classical Zen garden was added to the Tea Garden in January 1953, along with the 9,000-pound Lantern of Peace given to the city at that time by the Japanese government as a gesture of reconciliation.

Three spectacular, authentically crafted wooden gates (*Tori-no-mon*) were erected without nails in 1985 to replace others along Tea Garden Drive. They were crafted of Japanese Hinoki cypress by a crew of Japanese craftsmen trained in the art of traditional carpentry. Tea Garden Drive was renamed Hagiwara Tea Garden Drive in 1986.

Added to the garden on March 26, 1974, was the Hagiwara Family Monument, created by San Francisco artist Ruth Asawa as a tribute to the family that had created and cared for the garden for some 40 years. Near the bronze plaque, mounted on a boulder selected from the Sierra Nevada, is a small frog that answers the frogs on the main plaque. Ironically, the work was commissioned by the members of the John McLaren Society, a watchdog group against park development.

Located just outside and west of the garden's main entrance is a stone lantern donated by the Federation of Economic Organizations of Japan and dedicated in September 1969. A nearby companion bronze plaque donated by the Committee for Japan Week in San Francisco is dedicated to the pioneers who emigrated from Japan during the previous 100 years.

Well-known oriental art importer George Turner Marsh, believed by some to have developed the garden, opened

San Francisco's first store for Asian arts, the House of Marsh's, on Sutter Street in 1875. Marsh was also a real estate developer, most notably of the Richmond District, the area north of the park. The Australian-born Marsh, a backer of the Midwinter Fair, was fluent in Japanese and had lived in Japan for many years. His involvement in the fair seems to have been as leaseholder and administrator of the Japanese Village exhibit rather than as the primary designer, as was touted for many years. For more information about this subject, see Tanso Ishihara and Gloria Wickham's publication *The Japanese Tea Garden in Golden Gate Park (1893–1942)*, self-published in 1979.

The Tea Garden has its roots in the Japonesque craze that began in 1853 when Japan opened trade relations with the West. The craze caught on after a stunning display of Japanese art and architecture at the 1876 Centennial International Exhibition in Philadelphia. Gilbert and Sullivan's *The Mikado* (1885) satirized the Victorian mania for all things in the Japanese style. Thanks to the predilections of the fashion-conscious and the need for something new, many of the upper class had exotic rooms in their homes; Oriental-inspired rooms were especially desirable.

General information: *415/752-4227.* Hours: *9:00 A.M.–6:30 P.M. or dusk.* Fee: *Adults, $3.50; children under 12, $1.25; seniors over 65, $1.25.*

74 William Randolph Hearst and the Ill-Fated Stones of Santa Maria de Ovila

If Orson Welles's 1941 movie *Citizen Kane* was about William Randolph Hearst, certainly the stones in the following story would qualify as part of the "loot of the world," described in the opening scene when the owner's estate is being tallied. What a loot they are!

Until recently, anyone who happened to hike the path from the Rose Garden to Strybing Arboretum's north gate would have encountered what appeared to be an overgrown stone ruin. Weighing some 3,000 tons in all, these gray, hand-carved limestone pieces—some of which can also be found along Stow Lake, in the Tea Garden, and even in local residents' gardens—constitute one of the park's most remarkable stories. It involves an abandoned monastery, a tycoon, several architects, a museum, an order of monks, the Spanish government, and many other parties and individuals.

The story begins in 1931, when publishing titan William Randolph Hearst planned to have the monastery of Santa Maria de Ovila reconstructed piece by piece on his remote family compound,

Wyntoon, some 250 miles north of San Francisco on Trinity County's McCloud River. The extraordinary Spanish Cistercian abbey, built in stages between the 1180s and 1600s, would have helped make Wyntoon even bigger than Hearst's other larger-than-Rhode Island estate, Hearst Castle, located to the south.

After a royal decree had decommissioned some 900 religious buildings throughout Spain in 1835, Santa Maria, located in the Castile Mountains of Guadalajara Province, had become a private farm. But the monastery remained until art dealer Arthur Byne found the elegantly spare complex in the later 1920s for the art-hungry Hearst. Hearst sent Berkeley architect Walter Steilberg to Spain to manage the safe removal of the pieces, spending the awesome sum of $1 million to acquire and move the segments to San Francisco, even at a time when the crash of 1929 had financially ruined many of America's wealthier citizens. Included in the bounty were a chapel, refectory, chapter house, arcaded cloister, and church door portal. In 1931, a total of some 10,000 painstakingly coded stones were removed from Santa Maria, transported on a specially built railroad, ferried on the Tagus River to Madrid, and taken to the Gulf of Valencia, from which 11 ships transported the 1,500 wooden crates to America.

Borrowed Culture

The latter half of the 19th century in the United States has been called a time of "borrowed culture," referring to the fact that no true new design aesthetic existed. While finding their way stylistically, designers relied on revived architectural ideas from many other countries' pasts to fill the void. The Midwinter Fair, with its exotic buildings, was a prime example. Eclecticism was the byword of the day: exhibits included the Esquimaux [sic] Village, with fake igloos surrounding a small pond; the Oriental Village, with Middle Eastern overtones (including Cairo Street); the Hawaiian Village; and the still-surviving Japanese Tea Garden, originally part of the fair's Japanese Village.

Outside of the fair venue, other park buildings illustrated "borrowed" styles, too. Some examples are the Moorish-inspired Pump Works, the Dutch windmills, and the classical temple encasing the carousel.

The crated stones idled for 10 years in a San Francisco warehouse located at Hyde and Jefferson Streets while renowned architects Julia Morgan and Bernard Maybeck worked on the design for a $50 million castle at Wyntoon that would include the ancient structures among its newer parts. By the time the design was complete, even Hearst was in financial distress, however, and the massive project was dropped. Morgan suggested that Hearst donate the pieces and plans to the city of San Francisco for a proposed museum. (Park historian Raymond Clary contended that Herbert Fleishhacker, president of the park commission, bailed out his friend Hearst and foisted the stones on the city as a "gift" after the board of supervisors granted $30,000 for the back storage and shipping costs that Hearst could not pay.) It was decided that the stones should become a Museum of Medieval Art, a prestigious acquisition that would rival The Cloisters at Fort Tryon Park, donated to New York City by John D. Rockefeller in 1930. Julia Morgan was again drafted for the task, her most important commission in the 1940s, and put together a plan in 1941. The bombing of Pearl Harbor Bay that December led to the eventual shelving of that plan as well, however.

Fires in 1941 and the following year,

74 In 1990, a city worker dumped a four-foot-tall solid granite traffic bollard in the park near the main cluster of Santa Maria de Ovila ruins. Hindu worshipers were inspired to claim the site, including the bullet-shaped bollard, as holy ground and pulled in some of the adjacent Santa Maria stones, creating a religious circle called Shiva Linga. A lawsuit by the city followed in 1993, but the religious group won. Eventually, the shrine was dismantled; the bollard was handed over to Hindu Kali Dass and placed in a Sunset District studio.

some probably set by vandals and aided by the flammable oily residue from the eucalyptus trees above, burned the combustible containers then sitting exposed to the elements in the park. Morgan and Steilberg tried to keep alive the possibility of reassembling the structures, even relabeling the stones, but three fires followed, and many of the stones fractured when cold water hit the heated rock. The worst damage occurred with six fires in 1959, by which time fewer than half of the stones survived.

Meanwhile, on a trip to the park in 1955, Thomas X. Davis, the abbot of Our Lady of New Clairvaux, had learned the origin of the stones and begun yearning for them. Forty years later, in 1995, many remnants were given to the 600-acre property of New Clairvaux in Vina, Calif., where the sun-drenched climate is reminiscent of Ovila's. There, some 150 miles north of San Francisco, between Chico and Redding, 27 Trappist monks intend to reassemble what is left of the abbey on land once owned by railroad magnate Leland Stanford.

In March 1965, the 16th-century church portal was pieced together and located on the north wall of the de Young Museum's vast Hearst Court—the only parts reconstructed to date. Stored separately in a warehouse, the portal had escaped vandalism.

The year 1980 brought about new interest, due largely to medieval architectural expert Margaret Burke. The Hearst Foundation funded two grants, totaling $40,000, to sleuth out the puzzle. Burke cataloged all of the de Young Museum's items related to the stones, then set the next step in motion. Without action from the de Young, she pursued moving the stones to the north.

Some of the remaining stones now reside along Stow Lake's perimeter (see site 83) and in other parts of the park. In an attempt to finally build something with these, New York-based preservation architect John Bero has put together plans for reassembly of the chapter house—but the $1 million required to launch the project has yet to be found.

Some other suggestions have been floated for use of the stones over the years—from creating a faux ruin in the park to using the stones as decoration along Market Street or in a MUNI (San Francisco municipal railway) station. Some citizens suggested returning them to Spain. The final outcome is yet to be seen.

75 Heroes Grove and Gold Star Mothers Rock

In a moving ceremony on Memorial Day 1919, some 12,000 people, many in mourning black, dedicated this grove to the heroes of World War I, which had ended just seven months earlier. A towering temporary obelisk decorated with many kinds of floral tributes marked the focal point of Heroes Grove during the glen's consecration as a memorial to those who had fallen. The *San Francisco Examiner* newspaper had suggested the grove as a living memorial to provide inspiration to the living and a sacred monument to the dead. The first redwood tree specifically dedicated to the heroes was planted on the occasion and topped by a small American flag. The triangular 15-acre plot contains symbolic noble evergreen coastal redwoods, also called coastal sequoia (*Sequoia sempervirens*), dedicated by the Gold Star Mothers organization.

Nestled in the eastern end of the grove is an 18-ton natural granite boulder called Gold Star Mothers Rock. This memorial is inscribed with the names of 748 local men and 13 women who died during World War I. McGilvray–Raymond Corporation donated the huge rock, dedicated on November 14, 1932. The memorial was originally intended to be between the War Memorial Opera House and the War Veterans Building, a complex in the Civic Center, dedicated the day before.

Gold Star Mothers Rock

3 STOW LAKE

Surrounding Strawberry Hill is Stow Lake, the park's largest lake and a serene setting for boating or strolling. Every point of interest in this area is artificial. The lake, with its undulating shoreline, imitates nature, just as Huntington Falls, on Strawberry Hill's northeast side, plummets down into the lake over realistic concrete boulders, creating the illusion of a natural cascade. Overgrown landscaping, including trees, shrubs, and flowers, complement the illusion. Photographic opportunities abound here; one choice site is the Golden Gate Pavilion, an exotic sight among the naturalistic character of the lake.

A wide variety of waterfowl can be seen throughout the year, and turtles that sun themselves on waterborne logs have long delighted and fascinated Stow Lake's visitors. Water-loving plants inhabit the water's edge and in some places create a hedge between the lake and the surrounding footpath. The highest point of the park, the summit of Strawberry Hill, commands a 360-degree view; an observatory once stood here, until the 1906 earthquake put it into ruins. Nearby, the formally laid out Rose Garden invites visitors to smell fragrant blossoms. A hike up the wooded path leads to Prayer Book Cross and a huge memorial.

▲ *First Stow Lake Boathouse* ▶ *Rustic Bridge*

76 Rose Garden

Until January 8, 1961, San Francisco had no municipal rose garden, although a two-acre informal one had existed in the park on Stanyan Street between Oak and Page Streets early in the century. Rose plant purveyors Jackson & Perkins provided plant material to instigate the current garden, and Assistant Superintendent of Parks Roy L. Hudson supervised the layout of its 1 ½-acre design. This was a joint effort with the San Francisco Chapter of the American Rose Society, which obtained additional specimen bushes from breeders and growers throughout the United States. Rose gardens were enjoying a new vogue: the White House Rose Garden was simultaneously being redesigned for newly elected President John F. Kennedy as an outdoor space to host special functions. Today, the park's garden contains examples ranging from a simple five-petal configuration of the wild rose to hybridized elegant blooms in a wide variety of sizes, shapes, and fragrances. These delicately perfumed blossoms are a universal symbol of love and romance.

Because the fog-bound summers of the City by the Bay are not especially suited to growing sun-loving roses, the garden's placement was crucial. Oriented along a former arc-shaped roadway, the site is sheltered from afternoon winds, and the rectangular beds are oriented east to west, allowing the bushes to catch a maximum of the sun's rays. Garden enhancements in 1984 included latticed fences to the west, with the triple purpose of being a background to the exquisite blooms, a windbreak, and a support for climbers. Concrete bed enclosures were also created in 1984 and several old rose cultivars, specially chosen for the microclimate, were planted where there had been a hedge bordering Heroes Grove. The centrally located circular bed features miniature roses. Members of the San Francisco and Golden Gate Rose Societies provide instruction to rose enthusiasts when they prune the dormant beds each January.

77 Thomas Garrigue Masaryk Bust

Located at the entry to the Rose Garden is a life-size gray marble bust mounted on a pedestal against a backdrop of rose bushes. Thomas Garrigue Masaryk was the first president of Czechoslovakia, a statesman, philosopher, liberator, and humanitarian. Sculpted in 1926 by J. Matatka, the piece was exhibited at the 1939 Golden Gate International Exhibition on Treasure

Rose Garden

Island. It was dedicated on its present spot in 1962, a gift of the San Francisco Chapter of Sokol, a Czechoslovakian gymnastics association.

78 Redwood Memorial Grove and The Doughboy

The Native Sons and Daughters of the Golden West planted 39 saplings here in

Redwood Memorial Grove

1930 to celebrate those who had given their lives in the Spanish–American War and World War I. A tract for the grove was initially selected between Sloat Boulevard and Ocean Avenue, but the reddish brown-barked noble coastal redwood trees *(Sequoia sempervirens)* ultimately ended up in this basinlike area of the park.

The Doughboy, sculpted in 1928, portrays a young man holding a wreath of laurel, a symbol of victory and peace. The $6,000 work of M. Earl Cummings was added to a plain 20-ton boulder on June 1, 1930. The huge rock had been dedicated on November 6, 1927, as an entrance marker to Redwood Memorial Grove. The statue was dedicated by the 52 parlors in San Francisco of the Native Sons and Daughters of the Golden West to commemorate the order's 39 members who died in World War I. Another bronze plaque was placed on June 3, 1951,

41 The byword "doughboy" refers to an infantryman from the Great War, World War I. Starting in the late 1840s, sailors were sent care packages containing a baked dough-based cake. The name is thought to have originated with the large brass uniform buttons resembling the cake.

The Doughboy

by the Grove of Memory Association, Native Sons and Daughters, to commemorate those who had died in both World Wars I and II.

79 Colonial Historic Trees and Chinese Friendship Pine Tree

A symbolic group of trees, one from each of the original 13 states, was planted on October 19, 1896, in a gentle 450-foot-long curving pathway. The grove, planted just east of the Pioneer Log Cabin (see site 82),

Reel Golden Gate Park:
On-Location Movies

The greater Bay Area has been host to so many on-location films, even since the early days of the medium, that it has come to be known as Hollywood North. Some 425 features, several of them blockbuster flicks, have been shot for the silver screen around the City by the Bay since 1930, and many silent ones preceded those. Although hundreds of miles north of the movie capital itself, the Bay Area has many Hollywood connections, ranking it third in the country as a site for location filming. As the setting for a wide variety of stories, from drama to sci-fi and comedy to film noir, San Francisco has appeared in films that have become its goodwill ambassadors to the world. Countless television commercials, made-for-television movies, and television series have been shot in the city as well. The park has been featured, or has at least had a cameo role, in many films portraying a variety of times and places, sometimes utilizing its nostalgic atmosphere. These include the following:

The Bleacher Hero, 1914, Jack Warner
In the Park, 1915, Essanay Studios
Dorothy Vernon of Haddon Hall, 1924,
  United Artists
Greed, 1924, Metro Goldwyn Mayer
The Adventures of Robin Hood, 1938,
  Warner Brothers
The Raging Tide, 1951, Universal International
Scaramouche, 1952, Metro Goldwyn Mayer
The Lineup, 1958, Columbia
Vertigo, 1958, Paramount Studios
Portrait in Black, 1960,
  Universal International
Take the Money and Run, 1968, Palomar
Dirty Harry, 1971, Warner Brothers
The Manitou, 1978, AVCO/Embassy
Time After Time, 1980, Warner Brothers
Charlie Chan and the Curse of the Dragon
  Queen, 1981, United Artists
Hammett, 1982, Orion-Warner Brothers
Howard the Duck, 1986, Universal
Star Trek IV: The Voyage Home, 1986,
  Paramount
Burglar, 1987, Warner Brothers
Class Action, 1990, 20th Century Fox
Heart and Souls, 1993, Universal
Tales of the City, 1993, Polygram
  (Great Britain)
Getting Even with Dad, 1994,
  Metro Goldwyn Mayer

In 1919, the park commission denied permission to Belle Bennett Motion Picture Company to shoot in the park. At the time, Commission President Curtis Holbrook Lindley felt that the park should not be used for commercial purposes.

was a gift of the Sequoia Chapter of the Daughters of the American Revolution. The group's purpose was to perpetuate the memory of those men and women who had helped achieve American independence. The ladies chose the grove's location at the site of the Midwinter Fair's Mining Camp of '49, an exhibit simulating a Gold Rush town and celebrating the argonauts who had helped create the metropolis of San Francisco. The dedication date of the grove was chosen to commemorate the 115th anniversary of the 1781 surrender of Charles Cornwallis at the Battle of Yorktown. Bishop William Ford Nichols recited a prayer as part of the ceremonies. Included in the exhibit was a rustic log cabin (not the same one seen today), which continued to be used as a toolshed long after the fair was dismantled. Each tree was supported by a festive tall mast surmounted by an American flag and a shield designating its home state. A silver trowel with a wooden handle made from a magnolia tree (said to be planted by George Washington at his home at Mt. Vernon) was used to combine soil from each tree's original planting spot with soil from famous battlefields. The Keystone State, Pennsylvania, with earth from the grave of the Marquis de Lafayette in Paris, held the emblematic central position of the arc form, flanked on one side by the northern states and on the other by the southern states. A cedar from Valley Forge and a chestnut from the gravesite of Thomas Jefferson were included.

Park Superintendent John McLaren had suggested later planting 32 additional trees within the area circumscribed by the arc to represent all the states of his time, but no evidence exists that this occurred.

Subsequently, on May 19, 1920, a bronze tablet mounted on a granite boulder was placed when Bishop Nichols reiterated the same prayer he had given at the original planting. The boulder intended for the ceremony was held up in Truckee because of a railroad strike but was placed later. It is difficult today to discern the original patriotic trees.

Before the Chinese Friendship Pine Tree is a simple, flat-faced, rectangular stone, rather grandly inscribed: "Tree planted by His Excellency K. (Kai) F. (Fu) Shah Envoy Extraordinary and Minister Plenipotentiary of the Republic of China to the United States of America on China Day at P.P.I. Exposition San Francisco September 23, 1915." As part of China Day at the Panama–Pacific International Exposition (PPIE), this pine tree from China had been planted in front of the exposition's China Pavilion to mark the friendship between the two Pacific Rim countries. Some 7,000 local citizens, many of Chinese descent, attended the ceremony, where the ambassador received a souvenir box of jewels from the fair's most dominant structure, the glittering Tower of Jewels. The tree was probably transplanted to the park after the exposition closed the following December.

After the PPIE, the park became the benefactor of the many commemorative trees planted during the exhibition. Park records identify a site called Exposition Grove, although its location is unknown. Only this tree is identified, implying that the trees were added to the adjacent area that includes the Colonial Historic Trees.

80 Willis Polk Rock

Just east of the Pioneer Log Cabin is a natural rock on which is mounted a bronze plaque that reads, "Planted by the Garden Club in memory of Willis Polk architect

Pioneer Log Cabin with the Willis Polk Rock

and lover of trees, September 22, 1927." Next to the boulder, Polk's widow Christina had planted a live oak nurtured from an acorn by Park Superintendent John McLaren, but the tree no longer stands.

Willis Jefferson Polk, a descendant of President James K. Polk, was an architect of considerable note. He started his career in the Bay Area as an assistant to Arthur Page Brown. Later, Polk became a representative of Daniel Burnham of Chicago. He participated in the ill-fated Burnham Plan, a proposal to redevelop San Francisco on an imperial scale prior to the 1906 earthquake and fire. Working in both commercial and residential architecture, Polk was appointed supervising architect of the Panama–Pacific International Exposition Company in 1911. His design for the elegant Georgian Revival-style Filoli Estate (1915) in rural Woodside was commissioned by water and mining magnate William B. Bourne, Sr. That same year, he ran unsuccessfully for mayor of San Francisco. His most distinctive work was the eight-story speculative Andrew S. Hallidie Building (1917) on Sutter Street, in the Financial District, whose glass curtain facade started a trend. Sadly, Polk didn't live to see any of the structures he designed for the park finished—including the second Beach Chalet (1925), the first Kezar Stadium

(1925, now demolished), and the Kezar Pavilion (1926). He died in 1924.

81 Pioneer Mother Monument

Located near the Pioneer Log Cabin (see site 82) is the huge figure of a cloaked woman with outstretched hands and two youthful innocents, a boy and a girl. The sculpture is a symbolic tribute to all mothers who braved the journey west over land or sea. The piece was created a year before the 1915 Panama–Pacific International Exposition (PPIE), where it was placed to overlook the entrance to the Palace of Fine Arts colonnade. The date of 1914 was significant because Congress proclaimed the establishment of Mother's Day that year. Phoebe Apperson Hearst chaired the Pioneer Mother Monument Association that came up with the idea of creating the piece. The $25,000 cost was funded from the pennies and nickels donated by children and by popular subscription, with the largest sum given by the Native Sons and Daughters of the Golden West. Dr. Benjamin Ide Wheeler, president of the University of California at Berkeley, wrote the inscription on the base, beginning "Over rude paths beset with hunger and risk she pressed onward toward the vision of a better country." The base, modeled in 1915, also has bas-relief

plaques depicting modes of transportation for the pioneers' journey west and whimsical, traditional-appearing moldings that are in fact cactus leaves, pine needles, and pinecones; its corners feature cattle skulls and daggers, symbolizing the perils some experienced during the long journey. Sculptor Charles Grafly created the main figure from a live model in his studio in Gloucester, Mass. It was cast by the Roman Bronze Works of Brooklyn, N.Y.

When the PPIE closed, the bronze languished in storage at the Palace of Fine Arts, its dress marred by graffiti. Proposals were made in 1926, 1928, and 1936 to move it to the park, but the park commission rejected each scheme. The piece was exhibited again on Treasure Island for the 1939 Golden Gate International Exposition near the Tower of the Sun and then was moved to the park in 1940 under the auspices of the Native Daughters of the Golden West, who really wanted it placed in the Civic Center. The statue was rededicated on December 8, 1940, in its current spot. Nearly twice life size, the sculpture sits on a more recent concrete pedestal.

82 Pioneer Log Cabin

This cabin, renovated in 1992, now serves as permits and reservations center for the park. The building was originally constructed for the Association of Pioneer Women of California, which was burned out of its Financial District meeting place by the 1906 earthquake and fire. Redwood logs were floated down from Mendocino County to be used for the memorial building, which was dedicated on October 28, 1911. The cabin was a labor of love for Anne McIntyre, a president of the women's organization, who worked with Mayor Patrick Henry McCarthy and James Rolph, Jr., to realize her dream. Governor Rolph and Mayor Angelo Rossi attended the dedication of an addition to the rear on March 18, 1932. The John W. Cherry family is memorialized in a plaque dedicated on April 21, 1934. The rustic interior has a fireplace and originally housed relics connected with California history, including furnishings brought across the plains or around Cape Horn. Some of the degenerating log facings were replaced during a recent renovation. The new logs were taken from the Sierra by helicopter so as not to damage the exposed bark.

83 Stow Lake and Stow Lake Boathouse

In 1881, William Bond Pritchard, the park's second superintendent, made plans for a large reservoir on only the east side of Strawberry Hill to be used for irrigation,

exercise, and pleasure. Construction did not begin until years later, however, after attorney William W. Stow was appointed to the park board in the 1890s. With a plan for a waterfall financed by Collis P. Huntington in hand (see site 87), Stow was able to extend the lake full-circle around the hill.

Contractor W. B. Bradbury lined the lake with water-holding tamped clay from the area near Turk and Divisadero Streets in the Western Addition. Completed in 1893, the lake was ready for the Midwinter Fair held nearby. It has three islands; the one across from the waterfall originally had a towering mound of artificial rocks with a waterfall cascading from the top. Because the islands provide nesting habitats for wildlife, visitors are asked to keep off.

On the north shore of Stow Lake stands Stow Lake Boathouse. Boats are available for rental including row, pedal, or electric motor. Bicycle and roller blade rentals are also available here, as well as refreshments. This Alpine-style chalet continues the concept of fanciful themed buildings sprinkled throughout the park. Built into an embankment, the exterior is clad with horizontally oriented wood siding in two alternating finishes. Decorative features include cut wood fretwork gables and sliding window

shutters. École des Beaux-Arts-trained architect Warren Charles Perry, dean of the School of Architecture at the University of California at Berkeley, designed the structure in 1946, and Wellnitz and DeNarde built it at a cost of $34,249. The funds were provided through a bequest from Lawyer Alfred Fuhrman, who died in 1940 and left much of the wealth he had amassed to be shared for the adornment of Golden Gate Park and the city library. Although many park projects have been funded with that bequest, a 1942 request to bury the

83 Huntington Falls is a good example, on a smaller scale, of an attractive feature made to mimic something natural. Fake rocks, some attached to smaller real ones, are scattered around the perimeter of the lake, mostly along the western side of the road encircling the lake. The rocks also line the ascending path to the lake's eastern end next to the Japanese Tea Garden; some have pockets to fill with plants. These were created at the request of Park Superintendent John McLaren—a strange contradiction for someone so aligned with nature. McLaren apparently felt that the rocks available were not big enough, so he had park workers create larger ones.

benefactor's ashes in the park was denied.

The chalet replaced an 1893 rustic log cabin-style structure demolished in 1937. That structure was designed by Arthur Page Brown. Curiously, Brown's first proposal for the site had been an overscaled, formal, rectangular, colonnaded, templelike structure—quite the opposite of the rustic one finally approved for construction.

General information: *415/752-0347.* Hours: *Summer weekdays, 10:00 A.M.–4:00 P.M.; summer weekends, 9:00 A.M.–5:00 P.M.; winter, call ahead, hours depend on weather.* Fees: *Rowboats, $9.50; pedal boats, $10.50; electric motor boats, $13.00 (all per hour).*

84 Roman Bridge

Linking Strawberry Island to the surrounding Stow Lake Drive, this sinuous, iron-reinforced concrete span is a complete antithesis to the later Rustic Bridge. Constructed in 1893 by Gray Brothers Artificial Stone Paving Company for $8,000, just in time for the Midwinter Fair, the 35-foot span derives its name from its form, a semicircular arch favored by the Romans in the many places they conquered. Architect Arthur Page Brown may have been inspired by the form of a similar masonry bridge, named Ponte San Francesco, in San Remo, Italy.

The Cataclysmic Earthquake and Fire of 1906

Impressive statistics define the singular Bay Area event that started at 5:12 A.M. on Wednesday of Easter week, April 18, 1906. Sliding tectonic plates in the earth's crust caused an initial 40-second-long temblor, followed by a larger one, later estimated to measure 8.3 on the Richter scale. The second earthquake lasted only 25 seconds, but it was enough to rupture gas and water lines and start a fire that continued for three days. By the time the smoke cleared, more than 8,000 structures had been destroyed, leaving about two-thirds of San Francisco's residents homeless. According to estimates, some 3,000 people died as a direct or indirect result of the catastrophe.

At the time, Golden Gate Park played an important role as a sanctuary. Within days, some 200,000 refugees were camping in the park, though shortly thereafter the numbers dwindled to an estimated 40,000. The army and American Red Cross managed two tent camps with sanitary facilities, one in Big Rec and the other in Speedway Meadow, which were replaced later by wooden barracks. With the Park Emergency Aid facility and the Central Emergency Hospital wrecked, Alvord Tunnel became a temporary hospital facility, augmented by 10 large army tents erected in the field next to the unusable hospital. Doctors and students from the University of California Medical School assisted in the effort to care for the wounded. The army set up a camp in Sharon Meadow, with medical and surgical wards and a dispensary and commissary. The Medical Corps transported by train its largest tent from Washington, D.C., with 100 corpsmen to assist in restoration. The tennis court enclosure became a huge food-supply depot for the hungry. McLaren Lodge became a similar center.

Individual camp names sprung up on the makeshift refugee homes: "Camp Contentment," "Hotel St. Francis," and "Camp Hell" were some. Initially, 9 out of 10 homes were crude shelters made from salvaged materials such as rugs, curtains, raincoats, and bedclothes. Class distinctions disappeared, and the rich lived alongside everyone else.

Creative methods of communication also sprung up. A huge billboard at the park's main entrance became a community tackboard. Up to a height of 12 feet, slips of paper, business cards, and letterheads were tacked, giving notice of loved ones' whereabouts. Buggies traveling through the park had notices painted on their side curtains inquiring about friends and relatives.

Three of the park's masonry buildings,

seismically the most vulnerable type of construction, suffered major damage. The Sharon Building's entire eastern end collapsed, taking most of the roof with it. Nearby, the northern gable and chimneys of the Park Emergency Aid Hospital also collapsed, rendering the facility useless. The hospital was rebuilt within three months at a cost of $4,000. Sweeney Observatory's two stories atop Strawberry Hill were thrown to the ground; a total loss, the observatory was not rebuilt. The Midwinter Memorial Museum annex was racked to pieces and the west side of the main museum building peeled off, causing

closure of that facility for 1 ½-years. The huge bronze Doré Vase tilted dangerously to one side. McLaren Lodge had its chimneys damaged and minor cracks opened in plaster walls. Movement of the Francis Scott Key Monument was so extensive that it was not fully restored until three years later, at a cost of $9,000. Spreckels Music Stand lost its stone cornice, and balustrades and the broad curving steps settled, leaving wide gaps; cost for repair of the stand was $15,000.

After the conflagration, the U.S. Life-Saving Service station in the park's northwest corner played an important role.

Station keeper Captain George H. Varney and his crew sheltered as many as 150 people at a time in the small facility, feeding and clothing them. Finally, after some 3,000 rations were issued to the hungry, the station's supplies were exhausted.

The park was scarred as a result of the evacuees living there. When water and sewer lines were brought into the park for sanitation, ditches were dug. Trees were cut down for firewood. The total cost of earthquake damage to the park and its structures was in excess of $45,000. Subsequent damage to the grounds by refugees and military personnel amounted to $174,602; in all, about one-third of the park's acreage required renovation afterward.

Mayor Eugene E. Schmitz said of the homeless: "I'm only afraid these people will never want to leave their new homes here." Schmitz may have been remembering that the park's acreage had been wrested from squatters years earlier. When some refugees actually did try to establish squatters' rights more than a year after the fatal event, McLaren and park workers pushed them out. The city did benefit in one way from the refugees, however: it hired the refugees to grade and improve the adjacent Park Presidio Avenue and then to begin restoration of the city's playground.

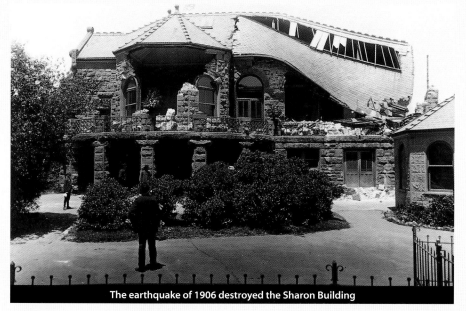
The earthquake of 1906 destroyed the Sharon Building

85 Strawberry Hill Island and Sweeney Observatory

Underpinning Strawberry Hill Island, the highest promontory in the park, at 409 feet above sea level, is mostly a towering sand dune originally blanketed with wild strawberry brambles and low scrub oak. Even before the artificial lake was created, the hill was known as The Island, perhaps because it rose so abruptly out of the adjacent land. The one million-gallon reservoir located halfway up the hill was created in 1890 to hold gravity-fed irrigation water. Steps across from the Roman Bridge provide a quick way to the top. Alternately, a spiral path provides a leisurely way to the summit. The hilltop was originally surrounded by what looked to be a rustic wooden fence made of branches. In fact, the fence was made of Portland cement modeled over metal pipe and wire.

The fabulous vista from atop Strawberry Hill inspired wealthy citizen Thomas U. Sweeney to donate $8,000 for Sweeney Observatory. A spiraling gravel drive up the hill terminated at the center of the 75-by-100-foot horseshoe-shaped building. The castellated entrance, oriented to the less windy east side of the building, funneled carriages into the building's center, a concept borrowed from the original Palace Hotel. The grand entry was reflected in a 50,000-gallon pool, which served as the headwaters for Huntington Falls. Two winding staircase towers that flanked the portal led to a viewing balcony over the entry. The outlook was so popular after its dedication on September 9, 1891, that an additional glassed-in second story, costing $5,000, was added the following year.

Sweeney was no stranger to hills: he provided the first local semaphore service from the crest of Telegraph Hill to signal the arrival of ships through the Golden Gate. He had arrived in San Francisco in 1852 with no money, but with time, he amassed a fortune through land speculation in the Sunset District, just south of the park. The wealthy eccentric died in January 1900.

Ransome and Cushing constructed the arcaded building, designed by architects George Washington Percy and Frederick F. Hamilton, of red-tinted concrete with the appearance of sandstone. One contemporary newspaper account boasted that the construction technique—of iron bar and cable reinforcements—made the observatory "absolutely earthquake-proof." The masonry structure toppled into a ruin during the 1906 earthquake, however, and was not rebuilt. A fragment

Sweeney Observatory

85 Shortly after the 1906 earthquake, a so-called scientific expert from Cincinnati, Ohio, declared Strawberry Hill the root cause of the disaster. Oliver E. Conner, Jr., claimed that he had strong evidence that Stow Lake (an artificial moat) was an extinct volcanic crater. Conner further stated, apparently in all seriousness, that the devastating event had hushed the "natural spring" (the artificial Huntington Falls, whose pump had failed in the quake) that once flowed from the side of the volcano (a very tall pile of sand) rising from the lake.

of the foundation remains on the southern side of the hill's crest.

When the second phase was complete, more construction had apparently been planned for the observatory. Sweeney had named park commissioners in his will, intending to give them real estate with a profit estimated at $10,000. But upon his deathbed, Sweeney transferred all of his holdings, including those intended for other family members, to his nephew Charles S. Brundage. The park commissioners and family members filed lawsuits, declaring that the dying Sweeney had not been aware of what he was doing. Two years after the Superior Court judge ruled in favor of the

nephew, the observatory was destroyed by the earthquake.

86 Golden Gate Pavilion

Looking like an elegant apparition, especially in the fog, the exotic Golden Gate Pavilion sits at the edge of placid Stow Lake near Huntington Falls.

During the U.S. Bicentennial in 1976, Taipei's Mayor Teng-Hui Lee visited San Francisco and made an announcement: he intended to bestow a gift upon Taipei's sister city—a gift that was uneasily received. The present, from the capital of the Republic of China on Taiwan, was a brilliant red-tile-roofed temple with a companion bridge that was to have arched across the lake. The intent was to confirm the friendship and cultural exchange between the sister cities and to commemorate the struggle and contributions of early Chinese settlers in California. Citizens requested an Environmental Impact Report regarding the addition of yet another structure to the park, however, and the outcome was

86 San Francisco's reciprocal present to its sister city, Taipei, was a playground similar to the Chinese playground situated east of Pagoda Alley in San Francisco's Chinatown.

a less obtrusive structure with a forest-green–tiled roof and no bridge.

Controversial from the start, the structure was finally dedicated on April 15, 1981, after a five-year battle with environmentalists. A score of lion dancers attended the dedication.

The octagonal open-air structure is a symphony of pattern and detail. The roof is a draped profile, clad in glazed, barrel-shaped clay tile, supported by intricately carved spandrels and columns painted in brilliant multicolor. A white cast concrete balustrade encloses the dais, and the same material is used for the bridge—a substantially smaller one than originally proposed—now spanning an artificial brook that flows to the lake. The design was inspired by buildings in Peking's historic Forbidden City. Bats (symbolizing happiness and longevity) and dragons (emblematic of good luck) adorn the temple, a favorite background for wedding photographs.

In 1983, some of the roof tiles started falling off, so the city of Taipei spent $50,000 to send experts to make the repairs. Further problems arose, and by December 1985, the structure was fenced off as a safety precaution. A sum of $200,000 was required to fix the problem. The pavilion requires periodic maintenance to keep it in good condition.

87 Huntington Falls

Park Superintendent John McLaren met with naturalist John Muir in the High Sierra Mountains one summer. Muir showed the superintendent several natural cascades set among groves of grand sequoias. When McLaren returned to San Francisco, he described his idea of an artificial waterfall to W. W. Stow, the wealthy chair of the park commission. Stow agreed that this would be a wonderful addition to the park and took his friend, railroad magnate Collis P. Huntington, for a buggy ride through the park, passing Strawberry Hill several times. (Huntington, considered ruthless by many, was one of the Big Four railroad barons and a former employer of Stow's.) McLaren joined them for part of the ride, but it was Stow who convinced the tycoon that water tumbling down the slope would be a fine addition to the park. Two days later, Huntington gave Stow a check for the anticipated amount of $25,000.

With skillful work by Stow and McLaren, the park did get its waterfall. The 110-foot-tall cascade started flowing on May 9, 1894, from its reservoir originally on the apex of Strawberry Hill—and then via a brooklet toward the cliff. The upper waterway was at some point abandoned, and water now flows from partway down the hill. Two wooden bridges, removed in 1999, used to allow aerial views over the length of the cascade, while imitation stones of concrete at the fall's base permit stepping just inches from the foaming white torrent before it enters the lake.

On July 25, 1962, the watercourse was undermined by a broken irrigation pipe and collapsed. The ruined falls were left in disrepair for many years but were finally rededicated by Mayor Dianne Feinstein on June 12, 1984. The reconstruction, costing $846,000 and funded by a state grant, involved sprayed-on and hand-molded concrete over stone-filled wire baskets, called "gabions," to create an entirely waterproof artificial hardscape.

88 Rustic Bridge

Spanning the south side of the lake, this charming double-arch structure is clad in massive red natural boulders, creating its rustic appearance. In contrast to the exaggerated ruggedness, dressed gray stones line the outside edge of the brick arches. The bridge was finished in 1893.

89 Prayer Book Cross

On a steep, 150-foot knoll, this 64-foot Celtic cross stands bold to the sky. The tallest monument in the park, it is nicknamed "Plymouth Rock of the Pacific." Here, above Rainbow Falls at Cross Over Drive, it commemorates the first-known use of the Book of Common Prayer in an English-speaking service on North America's west coast. That event is said to have occurred when English naval hero and explorer Sir Francis Drake landed his ship, the *Golden Hinde*, on June 24, 1579, on the shores of a bay in what is now Marin County's Pt. Reyes. There, Drake's chaplain, the Reverend Francis Fletcher, chronicled a service to commemorate St. John the Baptist Day.

The monument, with a span of 23 feet, consists of 68 huge blue Colusa sandstone

Prayer Book Cross

blocks. Bishop William Ford Nichols, the second Episcopal Bishop of California, dedicated it on January 1 at the opening of the 1894 California Midwinter International Exposition. Nichols had suggested erecting the cross and had found a donor to share his vision: George Childs, owner and editor of the *Philadelphia Public Ledger* newspaper. Childs was a philanthropist who donated many monuments to cities in the United States and England. He was instrumental in creating the original portion of Golden Gate Park's sister, the 4,000-acre Fairmount Park in Philadelphia, among other public institutions. Perhaps his boyhood interest in the sea drew him to the Drake project, but the persuasion of Nichols—himself a Philadelphian—was undoubtedly also instrumental. Tragically, the benefactor was not present for dedication of the cross and died soon after. The project had cost $10,000.

English-born Ernest Coxhead designed the cross, modeling it after ancient Runic crosses in Scotland, most notably one on the tiny island of Iona, County Mull, just west of mainland Scotland. The monument was originally slated for erection at the Pt. Reyes site where Drake is said to have landed, but the Golden Gate Park site was finally chosen over Drakes Bay for its accessibility. The monument's committee

rationalized that Pt. Reyes could be seen on a good day from the promontory where the cross stands.

Architect Ernest Coxhead designed many commercial and residential buildings in the Bay Area and was the unofficial architect of the Episcopal Church in California. Holy Innocents Episcopal Church on Fair Oaks Street in San Francisco's Noe Valley is one of his best-known works.

90 Rainbow Falls

The hill at the base of this waterfall was originally quarried for rock to pave the

Rainbow Falls

90 The park's landscape offers a curious aberration near Rainbow Falls. As the cascade's water leaves the pond, it continues westerly as a captured stream flowing under the Crossover Drive Bridge and finally spilling into Lloyd Lake. An optical illusion occurs between Transverse Drive and Lloyd Lake, where the greenery-lined watercourse appears to be flowing uphill.

park's roadways. The Park–Presidio Improvement Association requested the quarry's beautification in 1926, and by 1928, when nothing had been done, neighbors were beginning to complain about the growing eyesore. To resolve the issue, the park commission appropriated $17,500 in June 1929, and the site was magically transformed into an artificial gushing cascade, drawing water from Lloyd Lake. Inauguration of the falls took place on May 6, 1930, but just as important was the evening dedication of the lighting system on the following June 17. The name of the falls is derived from the arches of multicolored electric lights that once framed the cascade. The cascade is said to emulate one that Park Commission President Herbert Fleishhacker and his wife saw on a visit to the Bois de Boulogne in Paris.

WEST OF CROSS OVER DRIVE

Slicing the park almost in half is four-lane Route 1, the major north-to-south highway along the northern California coast. The grade-level roadway is so divisive that cars or pedestrians can cross at only two places—via an underpass at John F. Kennedy Drive or on the surface at Martin Luther King, Jr., Drive.

New York's Central Park had included transverse roadways that buried traffic from sight and eliminated the consequent danger to pedestrians. This feature kept Central Park intact while allowing road traffic to move through quickly. Golden Gate Park planner William Hammond Hall designed three such roadways in his original plan of 1872, but as work progressed, the roadways were omitted, with the exception of the Cross Over Drive Bridge. A tunnel or open depressed roadway to bury at least part of the highway has been proposed on several occasions, as recently as 1971, but not acted upon, perhaps because of cost.

◀ *Portals of the Past* ▲ *Towne Residence in Ruins*

91 Portals of the Past

With their grandiose name, these white marble pillars on Lloyd Lake at John F. Kennedy Drive conjure a romantic vision—but their history tells a tragic story. They once framed the entrance to the Alban Nelson Towne residence located near the crest of fashionable Nob Hill. The Colonial Revival-style mansion, built in 1891, stood at 1101 California Street, where the Masonic Auditorium stands today. But the elegant mansion, designed by famed architect Arthur Page Brown (assisted by Willis Polk), fell victim to the 1906 earthquake and fire, after which its entry portal stood intact like a lonely cenotaph amidst the rubble. Widow Caroline A. Towne presented the portal, along with some adjacent buff-colored Roman brick, to the park as a symbol of the catastrophe. Senator James Phelan headed a group that spearheaded the rescue effort, and architect Edgar A.

Alban Nelson Towne Residence on Nob Hill

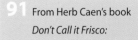

91 From Herb Caen's book
Don't Call it Frisco:

I never drive past the beautiful "Portals of the Past" in Golden Gate Park without remembering that somewhere in that area lies a dog—buried in a silver casket.

The story goes back to the mid-twenties, when Amadeus G. Langenberger, a wealthy art collector, had a pet poodle named "Boisie." One day, "Boisie" was run over by a car and killed. Heartbroken, Langenberger had a silver casket made for the poodle, and, one dark midnight, he drove out to the Park, and dug a grave near the "Portals" and buried his pet.

A police officer came along while Langenberger was in the middle of his strange chore, started to order him away, and then listened sympathetically to his story.

"Go ahead," the officer finally sighed." And I'll keep your secret. Nobody'll ever know there's a dog buried here."

And he was as good as his word—although his fellow officers used to wonder why, once in a while, he'd stroll over near the "Portals of the Past" and drop a flower on the ground.

Now, twenty-five years later, they know. Because a relative of Langenberger, deciding that the story—unlike the principals—should not die, gave me the details.

Mathews selected the site. The park commission accepted the portals on April 7, 1909. Ironically, one of the columns is now missing. On March 22, 1957, an earthquake measuring 5.3 on the Richter scale shook the Bay Area, the largest shaker since 1906. The eastern rear inner column crumbled. To this day, a wooden post substitutes for the column.

Alban Towne hailed from Charlestown, Mass., and started his railroad career as a brakeman on the Chicago, Burlington and Quincy at age 26. He worked his way up to assistant superintendent and, with the completion of the transcontinental railroad in 1869, became general superintendent of the Central Pacific Railroad. Towne rose to be second vice-president and first general manager of the Southern Pacific Railroad, at which point he built the mansion. At his death, he was reported to be worth some $1 million and to own about 30,000 acres within California, but he only lived four years after moving into the home.

The name Portals of the Past comes from a quote of the time after the 1906 earthquake: "This is the portal of the past— from now on, once more forward!" Poet (and later editor of *Sunset* magazine) Charles Kellogg Field found and immortalized this quote, while photographer Arnold Genthe's portrayal of the lonely portal in its original spot, framing the ruined city hall, became a visual icon.

92 Lloyd Lake

If history had taken another direction, this placid, clay-lined lake, known by some as Mirror Lake, might have been called Kissane Lake. The lake, developed in 1905, is named for Ruben Headley Lloyd, a park commissioner and attorney whose older brother was a notorious felon. To avoid any connection with her outlaw son, Ruben's mother had dropped the name of Kissane, and assumed her maiden name of Lloyd, as did her two younger sons.

Sculptor M. Earl Cummings created an eight-foot-high white Carrara marble stone bust of Lloyd with a bronze plaque on its base. Now gone, it was located just east of the portals (see site 91). The sculpture was erected sometime in 1913, a donation of the colorful Raphael Weill, the owner of the White House store— now home to Banana Republic—on Sutter Street.

93 Breon Gate

The grand portal defining 19th Avenue, where it intersects Lincoln Way, was dedicated in August 1923, a gift of philanthropist Christine Breon. Flanking the Cross Over Drive entrance to the park, the two square stone columns with

Breon Gate

M. Earl Cummings

Artist Melvin Earl Cummings created more pieces of sculpture for the park than did any other artist. He produced nine commissions, including the Pool of Enchantment statuary grouping, Brown Gate animals, the Sundial, the Robert Burns statue, the Doughboy statue, the John McLaren statue, and the tiger in the Rideout Fountain. Two other works are now gone: the Ruben Lloyd bust at Lloyd Lake and the statue of a child that sat in front of the Conservatory of Flowers. Cummings also sat on the park commission for 32 years, from 1904 until his death. As part of the five-person unpaid commission, which also oversaw the de Young Museum, Cummings fulfilled the mandated position of artist, a provision of the 1898 city charter.

Many other Cummings's works adorn the Bay Area as well. Working mostly in bronze and marble, the Salt Lake City-born artist won a scholarship to the Mark Hopkins Institute of Art in San Francisco, where he was a principal assistant to his teacher, Douglas Tilden. He was politically well connected with powerful individuals, including Phoebe Apperson Hearst (mother of the newspaper magnate), who, as a benefactress, furthered his study at the famed École des Beaux–Arts in Paris between September 1900 and August 1903. He also counted wealthy art patron Alma de Bretteville Spreckels as a friend. Later, he returned to the Mark Hopkins Institute to teach sculpture.

Pool of Enchantment before 1949 with sculpture by M. Earl Cummings

93 Curiously, a much grander gate, dedicated to the deceased Paul Breon, Sr., and his son Charles, was planned in 1898 for the intersection of Fulton Street at Seventh Avenue, where it would have displaced the 10-year-old Powell Street Railway Shelter. Its dimensions would have been staggering: 100 feet wide, 60 feet high, and 15 feet deep. But this immense gate—heavily ornamented with a guardian angel figure, life-size representations of the five Breon family members, and a pair of grizzly bears (California's state animal)—was never built.

granite bases have arches on the outside that welcome pedestrians. The Breons' wealth is evident in the decorative symbolic elements, including plaques festooned with laurel (the emblem of victory and peace), abundant cornucopias (Paul Breon, Sr., was a produce merchant), and lion's heads (illustrating power). Mrs. Breon chose the 19th Avenue entrance because of its proximity to one of her cherished charities, the 1923 Shriners Hospital for Crippled Children at the intersection of Moraga Street and 19th Avenue. John D. McGilvray, a family friend, was the gate's contractor.

Part of the original gate design included a tall column topped with a bronze statue and light. The column was centered north of the portal and stood on a piece of ground in the Y-shaped road intersection. The column and immediate grounds were removed sometime around 1938, probably for the construction of Crossover Drive. The gate is remarkably well scaled for the four-lane road now leading to the Golden Gate Bridge, but it was erected before anyone knew that the park would become a main thoroughfare.

McGilvray, who provided much of the dressed stone for the park, was born in Scotland of an old Highland family. He immigrated to New York in 1868, moving on to Chicago after the Great Fire of 1873 and then to Denver. He moved to San Francisco in 1893. His company supplied stone for several major buildings in the Bay Area, including the St. Francis Hotel, the Emporium department store, the United States Custom House, and the Stanford University quadrangle. His inventiveness greatly reduced the cost of granite construction techniques, leading to its increased popularity.

94 **George Washington Bicentennial Grove and Herbert Hoover Tree**

The George Washington Bicentennial Grove was planted to honor the country's

George Washington Bicentennial Grove and Herbert Hoover Tree

first president, on the bicentennial of Washington's birth. The National Women's Relief Society of San Francisco planted the sequoia trees, two of which were donated by the Los Angeles Parks Department, on February 22, 1932.

Centered in the grove is a large coastal redwood *(Sequoia sempervirens)* planted on May 24, 1935, to honor Herbert Clark Hoover. The Daughters of the American Revolution placed it to recognize the work of the 31st president in conserving the state's redwood forests.

Hoover attended Stanford University to study mining engineering and was a member of the university's first graduating class in 1895.

95 Elk Glen Lake

Imitating a wild setting, this reed-surrounded artificial lake was named for the enclosure that housed the park's first pair of Roosevelt elk, given in 1890 by Alvinza Hayward, a business associate of banker William Ralston's. The lake was created in 1936, with a capacity of

95 The shrewd Park Superintendent John McLaren initiated the concept of using resources at hand, especially for water, the lifeblood of the park. When a sewer link between Lincoln Avenue and Fulton Street was built just after 1906, McLaren tapped into the line and diverted the wastewater. Crossing the park at 20th Avenue, the precious irrigation water could also be used to fill the park's lakes, traveling through gravity flumes and ditches toward the western end. Neighbors' complaints of the noxious smell led to the practice of treating the water around 1912.

2.064 million gallons, as a holding pond for treated sewage water. Nearby was a water reclamation plant built in 1932 to treat sewage water to supplement park irrigation. The Urban Forestry Center now uses the plant site.

96 Mallard Lake

The overgrown Mallard Lake, one of the park's few natural bodies of water, is a favorite of waterfowl. A modest artificial waterfall, approved by the park commission in 1938, babbles at the lake's east end. Stepping-stones cross the stream to the densely wooded, idyllic south side of the lake. Workers for the 1894 Midwinter

Mallard Lake

Fair used the banks of the lake as a resting place during lunch breaks and affectionately called it "Hobo Lake."

97 Metson Lake

A decrepit artificial cascade tumbles from an artificial rise at the eastern end into Metson Lake, which is inhabited by turtles. Exiting the lake's opposite end, the babbling stream culminates in a marsh at the intersection of Middle Drive West and Metson Road. The artificial lake cost $9,513 to construct and was dedicated on April 11, 1908, as an irrigation reservoir that received its water supply from the Murphy Windmill. Its namesake, William Henry Metson, was president of the park commission, a lawyer, a Sacramento delta farmer, and a Yosemite park commissioner.

98 Speedway Meadow

Long, lush Speedway Meadow is all that remains of the old Speed Road that ran diagonally from where John F. Kennedy Drive meets Lloyd Lake to a point just before 41st Avenue, where it turned north. Its straightaway allowed drivers to reach exciting speeds on horses and, later, with the newfangled horseless carriage. The 1 1/4-mile-long speedway was graded and surfaced with clay in 1888 at a cost of $32,500, a gift to the park from private donors, including such well-known

> 98 San Francisco mounted patrol officers in 1900 were required to pass a rigorous test to demonstrate their riding skills, an examination not for the faint. With a steed sporting a Spanish saddle, the rookie had to ride at breakneck pace down the old speedway track and pick up a handkerchief from the ground while at full gallop. A more difficult exercise was to pluck a person from the back of a runaway horse or to secure a lariat over the head of a speeding bicyclist.

individuals as Leland Stanford, Charles Crocker, Adolph Sutro, and A. B. Spreckels. The 100-foot-wide track was divided down the middle with a hedge to facilitate racing in either direction. By 1903, the neglected roadbed was unusable; the speedway was erased by 1906. The meadow was improved in 1936 with the aid of Works Progress Administration funds.

A remnant of the speedway, on the west side of the stadium, is called Little Speedway Meadow.

99 Marx Meadow

Many park visitors wonder if Karl Marx was the namesake for this troughlike glade, but in fact, it was named for Johanne Augusta Emily Marx of Napa. Of an estate totaling $200,000 when she died

in 1914, she willed $5,000 to the park for general improvements. Marx is a true meadow in wet months of the year, sometimes submerged. The adjacent path is what remains of a roadway that was closed in 1982.

100 Beardslee Gate

In 1953, a simple cast concrete gateway with benches was erected at the intersection of Fulton Street and the 30th Avenue entry to the park. The structure is modest but comes with an interesting story. A San Francisco character known as "the Witch of Powell Street" funded the gate. Mary Taylor Beardslee, a widow known about town mainly as a reclusive resident of the Sir Francis Drake Hotel, always wore a black, shroudlike outfit and rarely spoke to anyone unless forced to. When the 77-year-old Beardslee died in 1946, she stipulated that the exact amount of $12,113.08 be used to build a memorial at the 24th Avenue park entrance at Fulton Street. This was to honor her father, Thomas Gibbons Taylor (a captain in the Union Navy during the Civil War) and her mother, Sarah Casebolt Taylor. The park commission did not honor the desired location but compromised with the 30th Avenue location. The money was also used to widen the Brown Gate at Eighth Avenue.

5
GOLDEN GATE PARK STADIUM

Golden Gate Park Stadium, the largest park structure, is the core of this area devoted primarily to active outdoor sports. Soccer, jogging, fly-casting, horse riding, and pétanque (a French outdoor bowling game) all occur here among the forests. Model yachting is the key (and only authorized) activity, usually on weekends, on Spreckels Lake, the major water feature here. Nearby, bison roam lazily in their large, grassy paddock. Many off-the-beaten-track paths thread through the densely wooded area. Several of the structures here are products of the Works Progress Administration (WPA) era, a part of President Franklin Roosevelt's "New Deal" intended to provide jobs. Statues do not exist in this part of the park.

▲ *Polo game being played at Golden Gate Park May 1, 1948*   ▶ *Horse stalls*

Flora: The Essence of the Park

Look for fantastically gnarled tree trunks with stringy, paperlike bark proliferating throughout the park, especially along John F. Kennedy Drive. Captain John Cook's crew discovered that the leaves of this species of Australian tea tree *(Leptospermum laevigatum)* had a fine flavor when used to brew tea. Park Superintendent John McLaren planted the horizontally growing species, one of the first trees introduced into California, throughout the park's dunes, along with other plants to hold the sand in place.

During the 1980s, a weed known as the South African capeweed *(Arctotheca calendula)* began proliferating on the park's grounds. Dubbed Johnny Weedseed, an unemployed mechanical engineer was accused, although not convicted, of dispersing this botanical pest, which smothers all other adjacent plant life. The man was also thought to be responsible for planting the fast-growing water hyacinths that choke the park's lakes in some places. It's also possible, though, that the Recreation and Park Department introduced the capeweed as a ground cover during the dry period of the mid-1970s. Broad, silvery green leaves with yellow, daisylike blossoms identify the hardy, drought-resistant plant sometimes used along freeways.

101 Lindley Meadow

This sunken meadow bordering John F. Kennedy Drive is a pleasant place to host large picnics. It was named in 1918 to honor Curtis Holbrook Lindley, a park commission president.

The meadow was once the site of an annual Christmas Nativity tableau depicting the birth of Christ in life-size figures, flanked by live grazing sheep. Not just accidental participants in a holiday pageant, the sheep were also used to shear the grass, replicating President Woodrow Wilson's practice of keeping sheep on the White House lawn. The lawn mowers had unusually nice circumstances: they were tended by a shepherd, enjoyed high-quality clover and bluegrass, were groomed and washed twice a week, and slept in a warmed arbor. In 1926, some 800 pounds of their shorn wool brought the park $252 from the Pacific Wool Products Company.

At the east end of the meadow is a rise that used to be called Broom Point for the various species of broom shrub that grew there.

A 26-foot-high carved totem once decorated the southern rise of the meadow, opposite the 30th Avenue entrance road. The monumental artwork, erected in 1941 and titled *Goddess of the Forest*, was created by wood sculptor

Dudley C. Carter for the Golden Gate International Exposition. After the artwork was badly damaged due to improper exposure, the sculptor had it moved to San Francisco City College in 1984. A large concrete platform is all that remains.

102 Golden Gate Park Stables

Lessons in riding and horsemanship, as well as guided trail rides for adults and children with all levels and capabilities, are available from the Riding Academy. Horses may be boarded at the stables. The four central buildings with glass block windows were completed in 1939 as a Works Progress Administration project. Cast concrete bleachers, constructed in

103

"Army Day," held in the stadium on April 12, 1941, was in fact an encore of a performance held the previous Sunday at Fort Winfield Scott in the Presidio. Several thousand civilians came to the placid park to see the equipment of a war raging across the seas. Mostly recent recruits showed off their new skills, fired guns, and held a parade. Submarine mines, a defense specific to guarding the entrance of San Francisco Bay, were exhibited. Propaganda of this type showed off the might of the nation's war force.

1909 for the adjacent stadium, serve as a roof for the stable on the ring's fourth side. Equestrian trails thread throughout the western two-thirds of the park.

Location: *John F. Kennedy Drive at 36th Ave.* General information: *415/668-7360.* Hours: *9:00 A.M.–5:00 P.M.* Fee: *$30.00 for a 1-hour trail ride (reservations required).*

103 Golden Gate Park Stadium (aka the Polo Field)

The Golden Gate Park Stadium, the park's largest structure, plays host to many different types of events, for individuals and en masse. Here visitors can jog, watch soccer, or attend a rally.

Intended to be the biggest amphitheater in the world, the stadium envisioned in 1904 remained unfinished, in part, because of a lack of accessibility. The monumental design by architect brothers James W. Reid and Merritt Reid, estimated to cost $1 million, would have featured an arcaded enclosure interspersed with towering portals and enclosing seating for 60,000. The seats were to overlook a 30-acre field one full mile in circumference.

Only a fraction of the original plan was carried through, however, and the track area is just half of the planned circumference. Popular subscription for

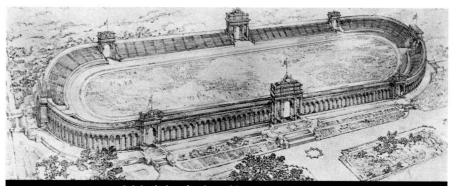
Original plans for the Golden Gate Park Stadium

103 One of the prime moments in aviation history occurred in Golden Gate Park Stadium. On September 11, 1911, 10,000 spectators witnessed L.A. pioneer aviator Robert G. Fowler as he took off in his Burgess–Wright biplane from the long, flat lawn. San Francisco Mayor James Rolph christened the plane with water from the Pacific Ocean. Fowler, who had been trained by the Wright Brothers themselves, was inspired by a $50,000 prize offered by newspaper mogul William Randolph Hearst in the fall of 1910. Typical of his genius for publicity, Hearst had challenged aviators to make an unprecedented transcontinental flight, parallel to the equator, within 30 days—with the stipulation that completion be by October 10, 1911. The newspaper sales gimmick wasn't exactly an original idea; the London Daily Mail had offered £1,000 to the first person to fly the English Channel in 1909.

An optimist, Fowler hoped to fly the distance in a short 20 days and was the first of three aviators to get under way, anticipating his first stop at the foot of the Sierra Nevada in Auburn, 129 miles away. Fowler's parents, assistants, and mechanics followed in a chase-train on the Southern Pacific Railroad, whose tracks were the only reliable landmark for navigating an airplane. The following day, Fowler approached the dangerous downdrafts of Donner Pass, but his plane went down near the Placer County village of Alta with a broken rudder-control cable. After crashing in some trees, he was mildly injured. Twelve days later, with a rebuilt plane, he attempted to cross the summit—but his trip ended in Emigrant Gap, and he never got across the California border. One of his competitors, Calbraith Perry Rodgers, did make a record-breaking transcontinental journey— 49 days and 4,231 miles later—but no one succeeded in winning the Hearst prize money.

103 The stadium became famous for the January 14, 1967, "Feast of the Incongruous," with 10,000 in attendance. The human "be-in" was a prelude to the hippie invasion of the neighboring Haight–Ashbury District during the famous—or infamous, depending on your point of view—Summer of Love. At the stadium, Harvard Professor and LSD advocate Timothy Leary spoke now-famous words to the throng, advising those in attendance to "turn on, tune in and drop out." Hippie icons Jefferson Airplane, poet Alan Ginsberg, and Jerry Rubin also attended. After many problems and faded ideals, the period ended with the "Death of the Hippie Parade" on October 6.

$20,000, much of it collected by the Amateur Driving Association, was combined with $25,000 from the park coffers to build the stadium, inaugurated July 4, 1906, soon after the great earthquake. The field originally incorporated a horse track around the outside, a bicycle track, and grounds designed, in part, for playing polo. Tunnels through the raised perimeter allow direct entrance to the field. A section of pleated cast-concrete grandstand about 100 feet long, inaugurated on April 3, 1909, is the only major part of the original scheme ever realized. The

harness-horse-racing track, dedicated on May 12, 1907, replaced the former Speed Road in part displaced by the stadium. The octagonal concrete judges'/starter stand, with its distinctive tile roof, was designed by G. A. Dodge to replace a more decorative stand built in 1908 with funds from F. H. Burke, whose wife, Mary, later funded construction of the de Young Museum tower.

In 1911, there was a push to complete the Reid Brothers scheme for use in the 1915 Panama–Pacific International

Exposition, slated to occur within the western end of the park. The exposition site was moved to the Marina, however, and the plan was never realized.

104 Frederick C. Egan Memorial Police Stables

Construction of the Frederick C. Egan Stables began in 1932, but a funding shortage delayed the process until 1935, when the Emergency Relief Administration announced its intention to fund the structure's completion. William P. Day,

Keeping the horses clean at Frederick C. Egan Memorial Police Stables

Weather vane on Egan Stables

105 Anglers Lodge and Fly-Casting Pools

The Golden Gate Angling and Casting Club, originated in 1896 as the San Francisco Fly-Casting Club, built its first clubhouse at Stow Lake, where it also held practice and tournaments. The current clubhouse, erected with the help of Works Progress Administration-financed labor, is a charming, rustic cottage of redwood and field stone incorporating hand-hewn window frames and wrought iron. The leaded glass panel depicting a fishing fly came from the front door of the 1928 lodge that had perched on the edge of Stow Lake, replacing its predecessor. Three huge, shallow, concrete-lined tanks provide a variety of targets for casting practice—but no live fish. The pools were dedicated on February 22, 1938, the same day the cornerstone for the lodge was laid. The lodge was dedicated on March 5, 1939.

General information: 415/386-2630.

106 Spreckels Lake and San Francisco Model Yacht Club

Landlubbers have the opportunity to test their seamanship with power- and

of the architectural firm Weeks and Day, designed the elegant, cupola-topped barn. The T-shaped, stucco, two-story structure received a sympathetic addition to the east side in 1996. Fred Egan, for whom the stables were named, was a long-time horse trainer for the police department.

Across from the Egan Stables stands a green-painted cast iron double bowl fountain for horses. It was donated by the San Francisco Society for the Prevention of Cruelty to Animals to honor Sargent Edward Cantwell, a mounted horse police officer and horse trainer.

Casting at the Anglers Lodge

sailboats at this shallow, artificial lake. The park's second largest lake, with a capacity of 7.81 million gallons, was the 1902 brainchild of the Model Yacht Club after its members experienced conflicts with real boats on Stow Lake. Fresh water from the wells of the Dutch Windmill started flowing on January 14, 1904, into the basin, initially used as an irrigation overflow reservoir. The lake's shape—fairly straight on the north side and undulating elsewhere—allows the skippers of free-sail boats to maneuver them easily along the Fulton Street side. A giant concrete turtle resides in the lake's west end, acting as an island for the terrapin to catch the sun's warming rays. The lake was named for then-Park Commission Board President Adolph Bernard Spreckels.

The San Francisco Model Yacht Club has its origins in late-19th-century San Francisco, when miniature boats were sailed off Meiggs' Long Wharf in San

106 The "Little St. Francis" took its name from the Hotel St. Francis, only two years old when the 1906 fire gutted it. The temporary facility opened across the street from the original in Union Square just 40 days after the frightening event. Classically styled, the white-painted wood building fronted Powell Street on the west side of the square and sported a portico of paired columns flanked by plainer two-story wings with 110 guest rooms. In 1907, when the newly renovated hotel was ready for occupancy, the makeshift hotel was removed.

Francisco Bay. The club was first organized at Stow Lake in 1898 and moved to the new Spreckels Lake in 1904 after park commissioners granted the club exclusive use of the lake for model boating. The prior clubhouse was the recycled front portion of the colonial-styled "Little St. Francis," a hotel temporarily constructed in Union Square following the disastrous 1906 earthquake. The structure was moved in 1907 to where the stables stand today and was shared there with stadium users.

The current stucco, tile-roofed, Deco-style clubhouse—a Works Progress Administration project—was formally opened on October 12, 1940. Porthole-type

San Francisco Model Yacht Club sailboat races on Spreckels Lake

windows punctuate a pair of enormous doors that open into an entry with a multicolor terrazzo floor in a Moderne design suggestive of sailing. The functional interior consists of an expansive room naturally illuminated through glass-block windows. Much of the space is devoted to the drydock storage of sailboats, with a forest of sails like that in a real marina. Two symmetrical wings contain an office and a galley. In the center of the galley is what looks like a waist-high green-glazed tiled bathtub but which has a specific function: to establish a waterline location on a boat's hull when the basin is filled with water. The building is open to the public when members are there (on an erratic schedule).

The Model Yacht Club's season extends from March through the end of October, and its mostly male membership is equally split between powerboaters and sailboaters—affectionately known to all sailors, model or full size, as stinkpots and ragtops. Some boats are modeled after hull designs of real yachts, sharing their speedy, award-winning attributes. The club, the second oldest model yacht club in the nation, is open to all who wish to join in the camaraderie and are interested in many kinds of watercraft, especially on opening day in the spring when most members congregate. One current model

Senior Center

boater is a third-generation club member.

General information: *415/386-1037.*
Web site: *sfmyc.org.*

107　Senior Center

Living its third life, this handsome, Mission-style structure faces the intersection of Fulton Street and 37th Avenue. The stucco-clad design, a classic composition capped with a terra-cotta tile roof, is by William P. Day of Weeks and Day. A variety of activities, from active to sedate, are held here. Anyone over age 55 is welcome to participate in classes covering art, music, exercise, dance, and nutrition, just some of the many things to keep seniors on their toes.

The building opened as the Golden Gate Park District Police Station on March 28, 1932, initiated as a money-saving proposal to consolidate stations in the Depression era. The building housed District 14, Company "O," half of which was a mounted police patrol. Park Superintendent John McLaren was said to have shrewdly maneuvered the siting, intending the building to stop the Public Works Department from extending Sunset Boulevard northward through the park to Lincoln Park. The Board of Police Commissioners adopted a resolution in August 1937 to abandon the station—only to rededicate it as the San Francisco Police Academy on October 15, 1937. Later, in 1963, the building was decommissioned by the Police Department.

The Recreation and Park Department approved a new structure for senior citizens in 1969, following a bequest of $450,000 by 85-year-old Leroy H. Vane, a carpenter who had been born across the street from the park and who died in 1966. Although the will was not specific about the money's use, its contents suggested a recreation building for senior citizens. The new structure was to be built near the Fulton Street and Sixth Avenue park entrance, but the 100-member John McLaren Society, a watchdog group against park development, protested that decision. The abandoned police building became the resolution to the dispute, and the renovated building was officially inaugurated as the Senior Center on July 31, 1980, dedicated to Vane and his parents-in-law.

Location: *6101 Fulton St.* General information: *415/666-7015.* Hours: *Doors open at 9:30 A.M. daily; holidays, 10:00 A.M.–4:00 P.M.* Fees: *Annual membership, $12.00; per visit, $0.50; some classes request a $1.00 donation to the instructor.*

108 Petanque Court

This flat court for the old-fashioned French bowling game using steel balls was installed in 1907. Older players of the sport still occasionally come here.

A large, fenced-in dog run is located to the west of the court.

109 Bison Paddock

Unquestionably, the most unusual sight in the park is of the huge beasts that roam the grassy valley along John F. Kennedy Drive. The park's only captive animals today always take new visitors by surprise.

Distinctly American, and a symbol of the West, bison (the scientifically correct name for the species more commonly called buffalo) once roamed the plains of North America. Educated guesses are that 40 to 50 million of the creatures existed before 1830, but with the westward expansion of the United States, direct and indirect contact with humans soon diminished the numbers. Creation of the current paddock in 1899 coincided with

Bison at home in their paddock

the animal's all-time low population of some 400 in all of North America. Only five years earlier, Congress had taken the first steps to protect the bison, passing a law to prohibit killing them in Yellowstone National Park.

The park's first bison were initially kept in the stables, where Kezar Stadium stands today, while their enclosure was being prepared. The first paddock, located at the eastern end of the park between the Music Concourse and what is now the AIDS Grove, was established in 1891 and at first contained a herd of bison purchased by the park commission the year before. Unfortunately, only two bulls and one heifer of the original five bison in the herd survived the journey from Montana. The park finally proved to be a good place to rear bison, however, with the first one born here on April 21, 1892. Breeding was so successful that, over time, several bison were sold.

The current paddock was established on December 12, 1899, in Zeile Meadows, named after Park Commissioner Frederick W. Zeile, to separate the powerful bulls from the family unit. Visitors could easily see the animals in their new home from the roads bordering the enclosure. The meadow was in earlier times shared with elk, sheep, deer, and goats. A tradition in the early years was to name the animals for Shakespeare characters or famous people, but when then-Mayor Dianne Feinstein and her husband donated a new herd in 1984, the animals were given Native American names.

The lumbering appearance of the humpbacked but powerful animals is deceptive: bison can be quite dangerous. In 1901, three males attacked another male, goring him to death and then continuing to toss the prostrate body into the air. Another incident in 1924 had a better outcome. In the middle of the night, 25 of the beasts escaped, scattering into the nearby Richmond and Sunset Districts and terrifying residents as they tore up gardens and lawns and charged automobiles. One person frantically called the police, mistakenly stating that elephants had escaped and were on the caller's front porch. The next day, police used food to lure the escapees back to their park home.

Today, the San Francisco Zoo feeds and provides veterinary care for the animals, while the Recreation and Park Department maintains the paddock with the help of the Watchbison Committee Project initiated in 1992. The volunteer group gathers a monthly work crew to weed, remove fallen branches and litter, and seed the paddock with grasses.

Animals and Birds in the Park

Over time, a kaleidoscope of captive creatures has inhabited the park. Only the bison remain today, but the menagerie in the past included deer, elk, moose, caribou, and antelope. At one time, donkeys gave rides to children, while goats and chickens inhabited an imitation barnyard, both located in the Children's Playground. More exotic specimens have included elephant, zebra, bear, kangaroo, emu, and ostrich. A spectrum of smaller unusual birds—including pheasants of many types, peacock, and quail—were all at one time part of the park landscape. In February 1927, Park Superintendent John McLaren suggested that the city find a better-suited site to create a zoo, and in 1929 the animals became part of the nucleus of the San Francisco Zoological Gardens, a project of Park Commissioner President Herbert Fleishhacker. The zoo's connection still remains: Golden Gate Park's eucalyptus trees supply tender leaves to feed the zoo's koala bears.

✦ FACING WEST ✦

Bordering the briny Pacific Ocean, the wooded western end acts as a barrier to stop the ever-present afternoon winds from burying the park with sand. Lush green grass carpets the forested areas in the rainy season, in sharp contrast to the parched ground cover of summer. The stately Murphy and Dutch Windmills, port and starboard sentinels, anchor the park's corners.

In 1998, huge boulders were placed near each windmill, at the road entrances from the Great Highway, to proclaim the park's name in lapidary lettering. The park's western end is an excellent place from which to watch the sunset and the sometimes-turbulent surf, with the vistas especially spectacular when the clustered offshore Farallon Islands are visible in the distance.

◀ *Queen Wilhelmina Tulip Garden* ▲ *Former rustic bridge at Chain of Lakes*

110 Chain of Lakes

Consisting of North, Middle, and South Lakes, the Chain of Lakes was formed in part from freshwater swamps. Park Superintendent John McLaren envisioned picturesque bodies of water in the rustic style espoused earlier in the century by architect and landscape gardener Andrew Jackson Downing, who taught the notion of building with nature. Landscaping started with the North Lake in November 1898. A total of seven islands dotted the waterscapes, each planted in 1899 with a different species of shrub or tree to augment the grasses and willow trees

110 A grove of eucalyptus trees near the lakes was dedicated in 1919, at the request of Mayor James Rolph, as the "Cadenasso Group." Genoese-born artist Giuseppe Leone Cadenasso had arrived in California at age nine and had become a prolific and noted artist. Some of his moody Corot-like landscapes featured the eucalyptus trees at the lakes. Cadenasso hand-built his studio at 19 Macondray Lane on Russian Hill and spent his last 16 years teaching at Mills College, where he headed the art faculty. Tragically, he was struck by a car in Union Square on February 9, 1918, and died two days later. Sprigs of the Australian immigrant blue gum tree that he had memorialized decorated his casket and were worn by his pallbearers. The *San Francisco Bulletin* called him, upon his death, "the first California artist to catch the mystic beauty of the eucalyptus tree with a facile grace and atmosphere entirely his own."

North Lake, Chain of Lakes

native to the area. A gazebo once stood at North Lake, and rustic wood footbridges once spanned all of the lakes to get visitors to the islands. The bridges were removed to protect nesting birds, however, a great many of which still reside in the marshy bodies of water.

111 Jewett Memorial Bench

Facing South Lake is a 12-foot-long speckled granite bench honoring Fidelia Jewett, a public schoolteacher in San Francisco for some 50 years. Noted as a founder in the rehabilitation of older people, she devoted her life to teaching and charitable work. The bench was originally placed in Union Square, circa 1933, for $2,000. But the park commission felt that it clashed with Union Square's décor and selected the current site in 1946, according to an *Examiner* article on March 26, 1972.

On the reverse side of the bench is incised "Lillien J. Martin 1851–1943. Guide the child, salvage the old." Martin was Jewett's friend and fellow teacher at Girls' High School at Scott and Geary Streets in San Francisco. Martin was also a noted professor emeritus of psychology at Stanford University who focused on rehabilitation of the elderly. A native of Olean, N.Y., she attended Vassar, embarked on five related careers, and wrote books and articles. She learned to drive at age 76 and drove across the country six years later to lecture. A biography, *Psychologist Unretired*, by Miriam Allen de Ford, records Martin's long and altruistic life.

112 Bercut Equitation Ring and Dressage Ring

Originally called Horseman's Retreat, this ring was renamed in November 1949 for Park Commissioner Peter Bercut, who had a great interest in horseback riding. In 1980, a dressage ring was constructed nearby in an area that had been the beach stables. That ring was enlarged in 1986.

113 Golden Gate Park Golf Course

The first U.S. golf club was formed in 1887. Demand for the construction of a park golf course began in 1902, when a public committee studied the idea and presented its findings to the park commission. Evidence suggests that construction of greens was begun somewhere in the park around 1912 but apparently was not completed. In 1946, the *Examiner* pushed for a course, and in 1948 the *Chronicle* followed suit. Not until San Francisco Mayor Elmer Edwin Robinson dedicated the 10-acre pitch-and-putt links to the cry of "Fore!" on April 4, 1951, however, did the idea become a reality. Golf course architect John Fleming, superintendent of golf courses for the city, transformed the rolling dunes into green links. The nine-hole par 27 course is a short but challenging layout with all of the holes par 3. Contractor George Paulsen billed the city $74,475 for the project; the bill was paid from the Alfred Fuhrman bequest. Architects Pollack and Pope designed the starter's house, also in 1951.

General information: *415/751-8987.* Hours: *6:00 A.M.–8:00 P.M.* Green fee: *Weekdays, $10.00; weekends, $13.00.*

114 Archery Range

Bushes of clipped California bay laurel (*Umbellularia californica*) form a hedge to divide the archery field from the extension of 47th Avenue. Here avid archers can shoot their quarry of hay-backed targets, a sport known all the way back to Mongolian conqueror Genghis Khan. The pastime was first organized within the park in 1881; in 1933, the first range devoted to the sport was constructed east of Golden Gate Park Stadium. The existing meadow was improved in 1936 by Works Progress Administration-funded workers. Then, in 1938, the Ahwahnee Archers group requested that the meadow be turned over to archery. The site is well suited, as a shallow rise of dunes behind the targets catches errant arrows.

115 Dutch Windmill and Queen Wilhelmina Tulip Garden

Some people might have thought that the park commissioners were a bit quixotic when they decided to drill a freshwater well so close to the salty ocean and pump it out with a windmill, but test wells dug in 1888 proved that water was available above the high-tide line.

Water is the lifeblood of the park, and at the turn of the century, the windmills were the heart, pumping an enormous amount of water using the free power of the wind. Prior to that time, the park commission had paid the Spring Valley Water Company $1,050 a month to supply water. Park Superintendent John McLaren seemed prophetic when he wrote an article, published in the *San Francisco Call* newspaper on December 25, 1895, about the ancient idea of using windmills to lift subterranean water for park use. The park commission approved funding and ordered construction of the first of two windmills at their meeting of April 16, 1902. (See site 120 regarding Murphy windmill.)

Mechanical engineer Alpheus Bull, Jr., of the Union Iron Works, designed the 75-foot-high structure, which cost $18,161. Five-foot-thick concrete walls at the base anchored the round wood-shingled structure, offsetting the tremendous

Dutch Windmill and former Millwright's Cottage

116

Proposed Ideas (Most Happily) Unrealized

Among the many projects proposed for Golden Gate Park over the years, a few have seemed to be pure folly. Several of these would have added yet more structures to the placid park or, worse, taken away parkland. Details of a select few follow.

Pigeon Enclosure. In 1965, the Bird Guardians League proposed a sanctuary for the enclosure of the ubiquitous pigeon. The free-form tent structure by architects Hertzka and Knowles was proposed for Martin Luther King, Jr., Drive, near the stables.

Selling Off Some of the Park. Citizen Michael Hirshbaum, nicknamed "The Mayor of Hayes Valley," proposed in September 1929 (just a month before the great Wall Street crash) that a strip of land two blocks wide for the entire length of the park's north side along Fulton Street be sold off for the sum of $50 million. Hirshbaum's scheme was to fund construction of the War Memorial complex. This newfound real estate would also have added homesites to the growing city, many with desirable backyards.

Giant Map. With an eye toward educating the public about California, civil engineer Marsden Manson proposed a 20-acre scaled "living map" within the park in 1893 at a projected cost of some $50,000. At such a scale, the area representing the East Bay's Mt. Diablo was projected to be 20 feet high. Manson, who had been trained by William Hammond Hall, envisioned trees and plants indigenous to the various regions planted in their respective areas, a precursor to the zoned regional plantings found in Strybing Arboretum today. Manson's original plan, in fact, was even more ambitious: the replication of the entire United States in scale relief. Because of the ambitious size, and perhaps because of a lack of funds brought about by the Panic of 1893, neither project was realized.

Site of the Panama–Pacific International Exposition. The 1915 Panama–Pacific International Exposition was intended to celebrate the city's phoenixlike recovery from the catastrophic 1906 earthquake and fire and also to secure trade through the newly completed Panama Canal. The site selection committee at first planned to string the exposition around the city, with part of it in the park. The fair was to be held on 562 acres in the western half of the park, where two long piers jutting into the ocean would greet steamships full of fairgoers. With the fair's location undecided, ground was broken in the park's giant stadium before an assembly of some 100,000 spectators on October 14,

On the day of the ersatz ground-breaking for the Panama–Pacific International Exposition, a ram was born at the Golden Gate Park Stadium. It was named to honor the president and subsequently became mascot of the fair. The animal was bedecked with a jeweled collar, which read, "Bill Taft, Mascot, Panama–Pacific International Exposition, born October 14, 1911."

1911, officiated by President William Howard Taft (who nicknamed San Francisco "the city that knows how") using a silver spade created by Shreve and Company. The fragmented approach was abandoned in the end, and the exposition took place at Harbor View, now known as the Marina District.

Exhibition Building. In 1951, a huge structure reminiscent of the city's Cow Palace was proposed to promote the area's manufacturing, shipping, and industries and to serve as a county fair building. A parking lot for 425 cars with a pedestrian tunnel connecting to the enormous structure would have brought thousands of visitors, along with serious traffic congestion—the very problem that later led to a substantially reduced capacity at Kezar Stadium. By 1954, the 45,000-square-foot $1.3 million project had turned into the much smaller San Francisco County Fair Building, the tame compromise that stands today (see site 61).

Skating Rink on Metson or Elk Glen Lake. In 1988, well-meaning Park Superintendent Barney Barron suggested that either Metson or Elk Glen Lake be enclosed and cooling coils installed to create an artificial skating rink. Barron was inspired by the recent victory of Sunnyvale's Brian Boitano, who had won a gold medal in skating at the Calgary Winter Olympics, and by his own visit to New York City's Rockefeller Center skating rink. Neighborhood groups opposed the idea, and it was dropped.

Highway through the Panhandle, 1930s. In 1937, the Department of Public Works undertook a highway study using Works Progress Administration-funded workers. Known as "A Limited Way Plan," the proposal was for a comprehensive system of elevated, depressed, and surface freeways to relieve congestion in the city brought about by traffic from the recently constructed San Francisco–Oakland Bay and Golden Gate Bridges. The plan proposed a depressed roadway along the Panhandle and a thoroughfare through the length of the park. These mini-freeways were to assure swift passage through the city at an average speed of 40 mph. A foreshadowing of the post-World War II

highways to be built around the region, they would become one of the city's most divisive battles.

Highway through the Panhandle, 1950s. On July 17, 1951, the San Francisco City Planning Commission adopted a late-1949 long-range master plan for a citywide network of freeways. The park found itself in the path of transportation progress, an extension of the well-meaning redevelopment of the Western Addition. The plan was to continue Route 280, the Junipero Serra Freeway, connecting it to the Golden Gate Bridge via the Park Presidio, which would have bisected the Panhandle. This set in motion a grassroots campaign. A private group called the Society for the Preservation of

Golden Gate Park was formed, and on September 10, 1953, the Recreation and Park Commission voted to oppose the move. With the emotional appeals of the public and after many hours of raucous discussion, the project was stopped.

Grand Gateway. Looking like a cross-pollination of the Arc de Triomphe (1836), and the Carrousel Triumphal Arch (1808), both in Paris, France—but with more curved flanking colonnades stretching outward like arms—this classically styled gateway was to be on Stanyan Street. The overscaled portal was designed in 1912 by architect George Adrian Applegarth, who had attended the École des Beaux–Arts in Paris. It was to have been erected as a donation of the Sharpe Estate.

The Grand Gateway

Panhandle Extension. Instigated in 1899 by Mayor James Duval Phelan (a disciple of the City Beautiful movement), a chain of parks linking the Panhandle to the city's Civic Center was proposed. The extension was also intended to inspire new development in the adjacent districts. The idea went down to defeat but has been resurrected several times over the years.

Municipal Railway Line through the Park. A bitter controversy erupted in 1915 between park commissioners and the newly formed Municipal Street Railway, which reacted to the city's growth by proposing new streetcar routes. City Supervisor Andrew J. Gallagher proposed a public transportation link between the Richmond and Sunset Districts, crossing the park next to the beloved Concourse and Japanese Tea Garden. Initially, the board of supervisors, with support from Mayor James Rolph and the Board of Works, approved the plan without consulting the park commissioners. Park commissioners noted that residential real estate developers merely wanted to feather their own pockets. Although alternate routes were proposed, as well as a tunnel, the concept lost momentum and was abandoned on June 5, 1916. Ultimately, in the 1920s, the city's first bus line was established through the park. The No. 1 line provided a critical link

Construction of a rail line through the park seemed imminent until sly park superintendent John McLaren made front page news. The *San Francisco Examiner* ran the headline "McLaren Fights Park Car Line With Blossoms" on November 13, 1915. In yet another battle with what he called "the rascals at City Hall", McLaren's feisty actions are part of San Francisco's lore. With the city's decision to build through what he considered his domain, Uncle John stormed into city hall and explained that if this project proceeded, many of the park's plantings would need to be dug up. The equally strong-willed city engineer contended that few, if any, trees or plants existed in the chosen strip of land. Some of the supervisors decided to go out to the park and see for themselves who was right. Accompanied by the park comissioners, the supervisors saw "a flowing line of floral beauty" consisting of chrysanthemums, dahlias, and winter roses planted among other shrubbery and trees. As soon as the bureaucrats departed, Uncle John allowed his force of 300 gardeners to go home and rest. McLaren's troops had sweated all night to make fools of the streetcar men.

between the growing Richmond and Sunset residential districts, supplementing the streetcar lines.

torque created by the force of wind. Giant 102-foot-long spars of Oregon pine, donated by the Pope and Talbot Lumber and Shipping combine, held sails to catch the wind, which pumped 20,000 gallons per hour to the top of Strawberry Hill. This quaint structure, originally known as the North Windmill, started pumping fresh water for irrigation by April 1903. The windmill also became a prominent reference point for mariners searching for the hard-to-find Golden Gate. In 1913, motorized pumps were added so that water pumping could continue even when no wind blew.

The windmill started a long decline in 1935. Electric pumps were used exclusively by then, eliminating any need for the sometimes-sporadic wind power. Having outlived their intended function, all of the windmill's metal parts were removed during World War II and sold for scrap to aid the war effort.

In February 1950, a storm ripped a spar off the windmill, and in 1953, the noble structure was recognized as in an "advanced state of deterioration." City Supervisor J. Eugene McAteer introduced a resolution in November of that year to launch a renovation campaign, one of many ill-fated efforts toward restoration.

Eleanor Rossi Crabtree, the daughter of former Mayor Angelo Rossi, began a campaign in 1961 to raise funds, hoping to save both deteriorating windmills. She organized a committee and gave lectures to 400 organizations. Finally, 6,000 donors combined with some $100,000 worth of volunteer labor from the Seabees Naval Reserve Unit Construction Battalion to make the restoration possible. The replacement spars came from Oregon—with a dusting of the 1980 Mt. St. Helens historic eruption coating them. After five years of reconstruction, restoration was complete in 1981. Today the spars occasionally turn, but not to pump water.

A picturesque millkeeper's cottage, with a roofline like homes in Holland used to have, was located on the rise just northeast of the windmill. Work commenced on the house in December 1903, a project of Park Commissioner Aaron Altman. The windmill and cottage made a scenic and delightful vignette, but the brick house was destroyed by fire sometime in 1958.

Southeast of the windmill is the remnant of an artificial pond partly surrounded by large boulders. Water flowed into the pond through a small artificial stream from a source atop the rise to the north. The adjacent bridge was originally an overpass for the Park and Ocean Railroad that ran along the beach.

Below the towering windmill is the Queen Wilhelmina Tulip Garden, where some 10,000 tulip bulbs planted each fall blossom the following March; interspersed with Iceland poppies, the tulips seem even more glorious and colorful. The bowl-shaped garden was designed by Roy L. Hudson and named in 1962 to honor the long-reigning queen of the Netherlands, who had died that same year. Tulips, the emblem of perfect love, originate from central Asia and Turkey, from which they were introduced into Europe and the Americas in the 17th century.

Dutch Windmill: City and County of San Francisco Landmark 147.

116 Former United States Life-Saving Service Station

Dedicated on August 13, 1878, the park's first life-saving station compound consisted of a water tower, a boathouse, and the keeper's house. The boathouse, a 1 1/2-story wood-frame Stick Eastlake-style structure, was a variation of a station design common along both the Atlantic and Pacific Coasts. (The house now stands near the corner of Cabrillo and 47th Streets, highly altered.) The station—the first on the California coastline and one of four eventually posted around the fog-prone Golden Gate—was operated by

Former United States Life-Saving Service Station

In the early years, Life-Saving Service Captain George H. Varney would drill his men each Sunday to keep them in shape for the frequent rescues. The dangerous exercise included donning thick white duck suits, removing a heavy canvas tarp from the two-ton rescue boat, wheeling the boat out of the boathouse, and hauling it over the loose sand of Ocean Beach into the rolling surf. Soaking wet, the men would put on their life preservers and climb into the heaving vessel. (Even today, swimming is not advised in the turbulent surf that hits Ocean Beach.) While rowing head on across the lashing breakers—and sometimes the crest of a wave—the men would point their bow toward their imaginary quarry. When they finally returned, they would capsize the boat—and then practice righting it.

the U.S. Life-Saving Service, now merged with the U.S. Coast Guard. It stood at the northwest corner of the park, adjacent to the Dutch Windmill.

The purpose of the service was to rescue survivors from the frequent shipwrecks. Initially, the stationkeeper was the only paid employee, aided by volunteer help, which delayed rescue work from the remote station. A replacement compound on the same site

survived until 1951 when, having outlived its usefulness, it was decommissioned. At the station's closing, Chief Boatswain's Mate Fred Hanson estimated that some 1,000 lives had been saved at the site.

The treacherous San Francisco (sand) Bar, located at the entrance to one of the West Coast's most important port cities, was in part caused by the booming growth from Gold Rush riches. It grew from hydraulic mining in the Sierra Nevada, which eventually silted the Bay and its narrow mouth.

117 Captain Roald Amundsen Memorial and Vanished Ship Gjoa

Appropriately facing the ocean, this tapered monolith was unveiled March 1, 1930, two years after Captain Roald Amundsen's death. In silent testimony to the famed explorer, the first to navigate the Northwest Passage from the Atlantic to the Pacific, it stands near the former location of his ship Gjoa. The shaft is modeled in size and shape after the bautastones erected in memory of Viking chiefs. The 10-foot-high rough-hewn red Norwegian granite shaft is mounted with a bronze portrait plaque, which also portrays the intertwined flags of Norway and the United States, by artist Hans W. Jauchen. The memorial was a gift from

the Norwegian citizens of San Francisco.

Captain Amundsen is best known for his voyages to the polar regions, one of which resulted in a legacy to San Francisco—the circa-1872 herring sloop Gjoa. With alterations in place to bolster the 69-foot-long ship's structure, explorer Amundsen and his crew set sail from Oslo, Norway, on June 13, 1903, and spent three winters in the Arctic ice of the Northwest Passage. The epoch-making voyage ended in San Francisco on October 19, 1906. Amundsen donated the ship to the city on June 16, 1909, and the city's Norwegian community took up a subscription to raise funds for displaying the ship in the park. Unfortunately, the ship had a rougher time on land than it had at sea; the 47-ton vessel fell into disrepair by the 1930s, due to vandalism and exposure to the elements. The Gjoa Foundation was formed in 1940 to restore her, but World War II interrupted its efforts. The job was finished with a rededication on May 14, 1949. A severe gale in 1960 toppled the uppermost part of the mast, and by 1970, years of official neglect had taken their toll. On May 20, 1972, the vessel was loaded on a truck and hauled to the waterfront's Pier 48, then loaded on a freighter headed to its native Norway, where it arrived four weeks later. It now resides at dry dock in the Norwegian

Maritime Museum in Oslo, fully restored.

Metal sculptor Jauchen was born in Hamburg, Germany, of Danish parents, famous artists themselves. His studies included four years of technical training followed by another four years at the Art Institute of Hamburg. He immigrated to the United States in 1910 and two years later began teaching his craft at Stanford University, the University of California at Berkeley, and other institutions. Jauchen garnered a gold medal for his exhibit of bronze work at the 1915 Panama–Pacific International Exposition. Jauchen's Olde Copper Shop on Sutter Street provided services in sculpting, ornamental bronze, and iron work. One of his noted pieces was an altar depicting scenes in the life of Christ, commissioned by multimillionaire financier J. Pierpont Morgan, Jr., for his London, England, residence.

118 Beach Chalet

The only major park feature to front the Pacific Ocean, the Beach Chalet, originally built as a pavilion and restaurant, has spectacular vistas. The current structure was preceded by the Swiss Chalet, also a restaurant, designed by architect William O. Banks. It was constructed on the beach across the Great Highway from the present Chalet in 1890. Being right on the water, however, it was often threatened by the

encroaching sea, most notably in January 1914, when the foundation was at grave risk. After a new facility was built away from the turbulent ocean, the original one was moved to 24th Avenue and Irving Streets, where it housed a Boy Scout troop until it was destroyed by arson in the 1950s.

The park commission allocated $60,000 to construct a new and larger facility in 1924 and appointed one of the Bay Area's premiere architects, Willis Polk, who did not live to see its completion.

Barrett and Hilp, the contractor, later constructed the Golden Gate Bridge. The two-story, Spanish Colonial Revival, hip-roofed structure opened on May 30, 1925. The new Chalet contained a public lounge, changing rooms for beach visitors on the first floor, and a glass-walled, municipally run 200-seat restaurant upstairs. In the early 1930s, sisters Hattie and Minnie Mauser used part of the unadorned first floor as an elegant tearoom, carpeted with oriental rugs.

Mosaic and fresco murals in the Beach Chalet

118 The Depression era (late 1930s) saw the creation of the Works Progress Administration Federal Art Project under the Roosevelt administration. The artworks created for the Chalet were just a few of the numerous WPA projects in the park intended to get artists back to work—called "make work" by some.

With financing from the Federal Art Project [a division of the Depression-era Works Progress Administration] and sponsorship by the park commission, local artist Lucien Labaudt set about decorating the first floor of the Chalet. During 1936 and into the following year, assisted by artists Arnold Bray and Farrell Dwyer, Labaudt covered 1,500 square feet of the walls with frescoed murals recording contemporary views of San Francisco. Plasterer James Wyatt provided the wet canvas for Labaudt's work, which could only be painted a section at a time before the plaster dried, chemically locking in the colors. With sharp attention to period details, Labaudt illustrated people, including Park Superintendent John McLaren, and places around the city. Banners, like keystones over some doorways, recite the words of local writers who capture the flavors of the Bay Area:

George Stirling, Bret Harte, Ina Coolbrith, and Joaquin Miller. Artist Primo Caredio executed the stone mosaics to Labaudt's designs, framing the doorways and creating a wainscot; and Michael von Meyer carved the three-dimensional magnolia wood stair balustrade and bas-relief column covers. The octopus tentacles entwining the balustrade, featuring deep sea life forms, are of particular note. Despite these artistic additions, however, the restaurant was not a financial success and closed in 1940.

The U.S. Military considered San Francisco a potential target during World War II, so many defensive fortifications dotted the waterfront. The Chalet was adapted as a housing facility for the coastal signal defense station located in the field just behind the Chalet. After the war, the Veterans of Foreign Wars leased the Chalet as a meeting place and bar until it closed in 1981, the same year it was placed on the National Register of Historic Places.

The city designated $800,000 in 1987 for infrastructure repairs to the vacant building, including restoration of the artworks, completed in 1989. A developer was sought for the site, but none met the stringent requirements set forth by the Recreation and Park Commission. With a $1.5 million grant to the Friends of Recreation and Parks in 1994 from the

118 In 1925, a grand 12 1/2-acre, 375,000-gallon freshwater artificial lake with boathouse was proposed for the site of the current soccer fields. Intended to double as a reservoir, the lake was to have been named for Park Superintendent John McLaren. One step to finance the lake's estimated $100,000 cost was a fundraiser held at the Tanforan Racetrack in San Bruno on Sunday, September 19, 1926. During the benefit, filming was taking place for an upcoming movie as well. All the city newspapers ran stories to build up the event, and San Francisco Mayor James Rolph, Jr., officially proclaimed that Sunday "John McLaren Day" at the race track. Two days before the event, a parade on Market Street, from the Ferry Building to City Hall, had featured 12-year-old film star Jackie Coogan wearing racing silks. (The MGM silent film *Johnny Get Your Hair Cut* involved horses and was Coogan's last film as a child star. He was later known best for his role of Uncle Fester in television's *The Addams Family*.) Despite great fanfare, some 10,000 attendees, and the raising of some $10,000, the lake was not built.

Even earlier, McLaren had proposed a saltwater pool on the same site. Though that, too, was never built, Fleishhacker Pool, to the south, eventually fulfilled his idea.

Lila Wallace Reader's Digest Fund, the building finally reopened on December 29, 1996, after 15 years of closure. Today it includes a park visitor center, a gift shop, and the Beach Chalet Brewery and Restaurant—once more giving the public access to its treasured artworks and a place to stop for lunch or dinner.

Self-taught Paris-born artist Lucien Labaudt came to San Francisco in 1910. By 1919, he had begun teaching at the California School of Fine Arts, and he later formed his own school of fashion design. A noted California pioneer of modern art, Labaudt's local work can also be seen at Coit Tower and in the museum on Treasure Island, a remnant of the 1939 Golden Gate International Exposition. He died in a military airplane crash in 1943 while on assignment as a war correspondent for *Life* magazine in India.

City and County of San Francisco Landmark 179. Location: 1000 Great Highway at Ocean Beach. Restaurant: 415/386-8439.

119 Soccer Fields

Four playing fields exist today for this popular sport. Additional field space may replace the unsightly former Richmond-Sunset Sewage Plant that was at the south end of the fields. This area was regained with the long-awaited 1993 opening of the Oceanside Water Pollution Control Plant located some two miles to the south.

120 Murphy Windmill and Millwright's Cottage

In 1905, while the arid city of San Francisco was just beginning to seriously look at its water-supply problem, the park was about to build its last water-supply project, making it self-sufficient. When the earlier Dutch Windmill proved a success, a second one was built, using the donation of $20,000 from wealthy citizen Samuel G. Murphy to cover most of the $22,000 cost. Murphy, president of the

Murphy Windmill today

120 In the spirit of the Roaring Twenties, the audacious Velma Tilden performed a daring feat at the Murphy Windmill on November 21, 1921. An expert swimmer and athlete, Velma took a daredevil challenge to ride one of the windmill's spars; she made 25 revolutions before calling a halt to the stunt. For her daring, she received $25 worth of bonbons and, more importantly, extensive coverage on the front pages of newspapers across the country.

First National Bank, was a philanthropist. J. C. H. Stut, a consulting mechanical engineer from Oakland, designed the structure. This windmill, dedicated on April 11, 1908, held the distinction of being the largest one outside of Holland when built. With a 95-foot-high, 55-foot-diameter concrete foundation, the windmill was 4 feet thick at its base. Its 114-foot sail-clad spars rotated on a shaft mounted on a revolving domed copper roof, supported by the tapered octagonal structure clad in slate. In an average summer wind, the windmill was said to be able to extract up to 75,000 gallons per hour with its six pumps, although 40,000 gallons per hour seem to have been the reality. The fresh water was stored in Metson Lake, a mile-plus to the east. Now dilapidated, the once-turning sails are silent, the rotting spars on the ground awaiting restoration.

When the windmill was constructed, the surrounding area was so sparsely populated that it was necessary to construct a Millwright's Cottage nearby for the mill attendant. A millwright's presence was required at all times to apply emergency brakes to the rotating spars in the event of a storm. Designed pro bono by architect James W. Reid of Reid Brothers, the two-bedroom brick Georgian Colonial with Dutch Colonial elements was built in 1909 by contractor Andrew Wilke Company for just $3,383. The classically styled front portico shelters, appropriately, a Dutch door. Today the cottage needs extensive repairs. Although once scheduled for demolition, it has been granted a stay of execution.

City and County of San Francisco Landmark 210.

121 The Pavilion

The Recreation and Park Department is slated to start construction on a new structure at Golden Gate Park, always a popular place for public gatherings, in spring of 2001. The 1,900-square-foot pavilion will be north of the Millwright's House, with a wide expanse of glass facing south toward the Murphy Windmill. The structure will be a showcase for sustainable architectural materials and methods of construction. It will also be rented for special events.

122 Vanished Rustic Stone Overpass

A charming double-arch trestle, similar to Stow Lake's Rustic Bridge, once leapt across South Drive (now Martin Luther King, Jr., Drive) near the Murphy Windmill, safely separating two transportation modes. Framing the ocean view while looking west, like a stereoscope card, the elevated span and ramps were constructed circa 1883 for the Park and Ocean Railroad, which ran along Lincoln Boulevard, curved northward to cross over South Drive, and continued parallel to Ocean Beach toward Seal Rocks. With the demise of the line,

Ocean Beach Seawall

Park Superintendent John McLaren's dream of a permanent wall to keep the sea from encroaching upon his park became reality on June 9, 1929, when 4,298 feet of concrete seawall—stretching the entire width of the park's boundary with the ocean—was dedicated. The fortification still exists, sandblasted by the winds of time.

the tracks were sold for their scrap iron content to make weapons in World War II. In 1947, the span was demolished.

Rustic Stone Overpass

Blair, Hosea. *Monuments and Memories of San Francisco: Golden Gate Park*, 1955.

Board of Park Commissioners. *The Development of Golden Gate Park and Particularly the Management and Thinning of its Forest Tree Plantations.* San Francisco: Bacon and Company, 1886.

Brechin, Gray. *Imperial San Francisco: Urban Power, Earthly Ruin.* Berkeley: University of California Press, 1999.

Byington, F. F. *Official Guide to Golden Gate Park of San Francisco.* San Francisco: Board of Park Commissioners, 1894.

Chandler, Arthur, and Marvin Nathan. *The Fantastic Fair: The Story of the California International Exposition.* St. Paul, Minn.: Pogo Press, 1993.

Clary, Raymond H. *The Making of Golden Gate Park: The Early Years: 1865-1906.* Second edition, San Francisco: Don't Call It Frisco Press, 1984.

———. *Golden Gate Park—The Growing Years: 1906-1950.* San Francisco: Don't Call It Frisco Press, 1987.

Day, J. *An Illustrated and Descriptive Souvenir and Guide to Golden Gate Park: a new handbook for strangers and tourists.* San Francisco: J. and J. L. Day, 1914.

Doss, Margot Patterson. *Golden Gate Park at Your Feet.* San Francisco: Chronicle Books, 1970.

Ellison, Joan, ed. *A Survey of Art Work in the City and County of San Francisco.* San Francisco: Art Commission, City and County of San Francisco 1975.

Gibson, Richard M. "Golden Gate Park." *Overland Monthly*, vol. XXXVII, no. 3 (March, 1901): pp. 734-765.

Giffen, Guy, and Helen Giffen. *The Story of Golden Gate Park.* San Francisco, 1949.

Greene, Clay M. *Park Development in San Francisco, Past, Present and Future.* San Francisco: James H. Barry Company, 1924.

Hall, William Hammond. "Influence of Parks and Pleasure Grounds." *Biennial Report of the Engineer of the Golden Gate Park, for term ending Nov. 30th, 1873.*

Lewis, Oscar. *San Francisco: Mission to Metropolis.* Second edition, San Diego: Howell–North Books, 1980.

Lippmann, C. R. *A Trip Through Internationally Famous Golden Gate Park, San Francisco, California.* The Printing Corporation/F. W. Woolworth, 1937.

Midwinter Scenes in Golden Gate Park. San Francisco: A. J. McDonald and Son, 1893.

The Monarch Souvenir of Sunset City and Sunset Scenes. H. S. Crocker, 1894.

The Official History of the California Midwinter International Exposition, H. S. Crocker, 1894.

100 Years in Golden Gate Park: A Pictorial History of the M. H. de Young Memorial Museum. Fine Arts Museums of San Francisco, 1995.

Pruett, Herbert E. *The Golden Gate Park.*

Oakland, Calif.: Pruett-MacGregor, 1968.

Scott, Mel. *The San Francisco Bay Area: A Metropolis in Perspective.* Berkeley: University of California Press, 1985.

San Francisco Civic Art Collection: A Guided Tour of the Publicly Owned Art of the City and County of San Francisco. San Francisco: San Francisco Art Commission, 1989.

The San Francisco Earthquake and Fire of April 18, 1906 and their effects on structures and structural materials. Department of the Interior, U. S. Geological Survey. Washington, DC: Government Printing Office, 1907.

Robbins, Fred Strong. *Facts and fancies of the tour thru Golden Gate Park, sightseeing, automobile or walking by Fred S. Robbins.* San Francisco, Calif., 1916.

Wilson, Katherine. *Golden Gate Park: The Park of a Thousand Vistas.* Caldwell, Idaho: Caxton Printers, 1947.

Witemann, A. *The California Midwinter International Exposition.* New York: The Albertype Company, 1894.

Much of my research came from newspaper articles (too numerous to list) including the *San Francisco Chronicle, San Francisco Examiner,* and *San Francisco Call.* The *Golden Gate Pathfinder,* and San Francisco Park Department, and San Francisco Recreation and Park Department's commissioners meeting notes were also valuable resources.

ARCHIVAL PHOTOGRAPH AND ILLUSTRATION CREDITS

Pages 8, 11: City and County of San Francisco, Recreation and Park Department
Page 13 (right): No. 1986.009, Courtesy of University Archives, Bancroft Library, University of California, Berkeley
Page 33 (right): No. 1989.037,

Courtesy of University Archives, Bancroft Library, University of California, Berkeley
Page 24: San Francisco History Center, San Francisco Public Library, and Moulin Studios
Pages 37, 80 (left), 98 (right), 102 (left), 105, 118: San Francisco

History Center, San Francisco Public Library
Pages 28, 35, 95 (right), 98 (left), 120: Courtesy of the California History Room, California State Library, Sacramento, California
Pages 38, 41 (top), 51 (right), 52 (left), 55, 96, 97, 113 (right): The

Marilyn Blaisdell Collection
Page 116: The Marilyn Blaisdell Collection and Moulin Studios
Pages 47, 56, 58 (left), 89, 125: The Society of California Pioneers
Page 90: Christopher Pollock